LAWS AND LEGISLATION

BANKRUPTCY EXEMPTIONS

HOMESTEAD AND FIREARM LAWS

LAWS AND LEGISLATION

Additional books in this series can be found on Nova's website under the Series tab.

Additional E-books in this series can be found on Nova's website under the E-books tab.

ECONOMIC ISSUES, PROBLEMS AND PERSPECTIVES

Additional books in this series can be found on Nova's website under the Series tab.

Additional E-books in this series can be found on Nova's website under the E-books tab.

LAWS AND LEGISLATION

BANKRUPTCY EXEMPTIONS

HOMESTEAD AND FIREARM LAWS

ROBBIN RHODES
AND
PETE J. LAMBERT
EDITORS

Nova Science Publishers, Inc.
New York

For permission to use material from this book please contact us:
Telephone 631-231-7269; Fax 631-231-8175
Web Site: http://www.novapublishers.com

Library of Congress Cataloging-in-Publication Data

Bankruptcy exemptions : homestead and firearm laws / editors, Robbin Rhodes and Pete J. Lambert.
p. cm.
Includes index.
ISBN 978-1-61942-381-7 (soft cover)
1. Bankruptcy--United States. 2. United States. Bankruptcy Abuse Prevention and Consumer Protection Act of 2005. 3. Homestead exemptions--United States. 4. Exemption (Law)--United States. 5. Firearms--Taxation--Law and legislation--United States. 6. Real property tax--Law and legislation--United States. I. Rhodes, Robbin. II. Lambert, Pete J.
KF1525.B35 2011
346.7307'8--dc23
2011045823

Published by Nova Science Publishers, Inc. † New York

CONTENTS

Preface		**vii**
Chapter 1	Homestead Exemptions in Bankruptcy after the Bankruptcy Abuse Prevention and Consumer Protection Act of 2005 (BAPCPA) *Carol A. Pettit and Vastine D. Platte*	**1**
Chapter 2	Exemptions for Firearms in Bankruptcy *Carol A. Pettit and Vastine D. Platte*	**89**
Chapter Sources		**99**
Index		**101**

PREFACE

When debtors file for bankruptcy protection under Title 11 of the U.S. Code, they may exempt the value of certain property; in many cases, this includes their homestead. In practical terms, to the extent that the property's value does not exceed the allowed exemption amount, the debtor may keep the property rather than its becoming part of the bankruptcy estate and thereby being available to satisfy creditors. This book surveys the homestead exemption laws of the 50 states and the District of Columbia with an emphasis on the amount of the exemptions and the extent to which debtors may choose between federal and state exemptions.

Chapter 1- When debtors file for bankruptcy protection under Title 11 of the U.S. Code, they may exempt the value of certain property; in many cases, this includes their homestead. In practical terms, to the extent that the property's value does not exceed the allowed exemption amount, the debtor may keep the property rather than its becoming part of the bankruptcy estate and thereby being available to satisfy creditors. The Bankruptcy Abuse Prevention and Consumer Protection Act of 2005 (BAPCPA) introduced additional limitations on the extent to which debtors could exempt value in their residences when filing for bankruptcy protection.

Chapter 2- The U.S. Supreme Court's decisions regarding the nature of the people's right to "keep and bear arms," as guaranteed in the Second Amendment to the U.S. Constitution, has focused some interest on the extent to which firearms are protected from the reach of creditors under either federal or state laws. State laws protecting certain property from creditors' claims may be used both in and outside of the bankruptcy context. Federal law may also protect certain property from creditors' claims in bankruptcy.

In: Bankruptcy Exemptions
Editors: R. Rhodes and P. J. Lambert
ISBN: 978-1-61942-381-7

Chapter 1

HOMESTEAD EXEMPTIONS IN BANKRUPTCY AFTER THE BANKRUPTCY ABUSE PREVENTION AND CONSUMER PROTECTION ACT OF 2005 (BAPCPA)

Carol A. Pettit and Vastine D. Platte

SUMMARY

When debtors file for bankruptcy protection under Title 11 of the U.S. Code, they may exempt the value of certain property; in many cases, this includes their homestead. In practical terms, to the extent that the property's value does not exceed the allowed exemption amount, the debtor may keep the property rather than its becoming part of the bankruptcy estate and thereby being available to satisfy creditors. The Bankruptcy Abuse Prevention and Consumer Protection Act of 2005 (BAPCPA) introduced additional limitations on the extent to which debtors could exempt value in their residences when filing for bankruptcy protection.

This report surveys the homestead exemption laws of the 50 states and the District of Columbia with an emphasis on the amount of the exemptions and the extent to which debtors may choose between federal and state exemptions. It also describes the limitations on state homestead exemptions in 11 U.S.C. § 522(o)-(q) that were imposed by BAPCPA.

The amounts states allow debtors to exempt in bankruptcy run the gamut. A few states (New Jersey, Pennsylvania, and Virginia) have no specific homestead exemption. Several jurisdictions allow debtors to exempt unlimited value in their homestead (the District of Columbia, Florida, Iowa, Kansas, Oklahoma, South Dakota, and Texas), but some states allow an unlimited homestead exemption only in specific circumstances (Kentucky, Louisiana, Nevada, and Washington).

In states with a specific dollar amount that is allowed as a homestead exemption, the majority of states allow an exemption that is more than $10,000, but less than $200,000. However, more than 10% of the states with a limited homestead exemption allow no more than $10,000. Only 10% allow $200,000 or more without imposing restrictions not related to residency.

In some states, the amount of the available exemption is dependent upon age or disability. In others, marital status affects the available exemption. Some allow additional exemption amounts if there are dependent children in the home. In a few states, the exemption is lower for a mobile home than for a residence that is real property. In New York, the maximum available exemption is determined by the county in which the homestead is located. Massachusetts recently changed its laws to create two classes of homestead exemption—an automatic homestead exemption and a declared homestead exemption. The declared homestead exemption requires written formalities and is of greater maximum value than is the automatic exemption.

Some states appear to use their homestead exemptions to address issues not directly related to the home. West Virginia generally allows debtors to exempt up to $25,000. That amount increases to $250,000 if the debtor is a physician with malpractice insurance coverage for at least $1 million per occurrence and the bankruptcy is, at least in part, a response to a medical malpractice verdict or judgment. Washington State generally limits debtors to exempting $125,000 for their homestead; however, if another state has gotten a judgment against the debtor for income taxes due to that other state on retirement benefits that were paid to the debtor while the debtor was a resident of Washington, the homestead exemption is unlimited.

INTRODUCTION

Prior to the enactment of the Bankruptcy Abuse Prevention and Consumer Protection Act of 2005 (BAPCPA), the amount that a debtor in bankruptcy could exempt as equity in a homestead was generally limited by two factors:

(1) whether the domiciliary state allowed the debtor to choose between the federal and state exemptions and (2) the amount the domiciliary state allowed as an homestead exemption. A third factor was added by BAPCPA in cases in which a debtor had purchased the property within approximately three years and four months before filing a petition for bankruptcy. Additionally, BAPCPA restricts debtors' options for determining their domiciliary state and, thus, the state exemptions that will apply. Prior to BAPCPA, an individual anticipating filing for bankruptcy protection might, shortly before filing for bankruptcy, move to a state whose exemptions were more favorable than those in the state where the individual was currently living and benefit from the more favorable exemption amounts.

This report discusses the federal homestead exemption, the effect BAPCPA has on a debtor's homestead exemption and, in Table 1, provides a survey of the current homestead exemptions in the fifty states and the District of Columbia. The table also indicates whether state residents may choose between the state and federal exemptions.

THE FEDERAL HOMESTEAD EXEMPTION

Section 522 of the Bankruptcy Code addresses the extent to which an individual debtor may elect to exempt equity in certain property from becoming part of the bankruptcy estate. Property exempted from the bankruptcy estate is not available to satisfy creditors. Among the exemptions explicitly provided in the Bankruptcy Code—the federal exemptions—are a homestead exemption in the amount of $21,625[1] and a "wildcard" exemption of $1,150[2] that can also be applied to the homestead if the debtor chooses so long as the federal exemptions are available to the debtor.

To the extent allowed under state law, the Bankruptcy Code allows debtors to choose between using the federal exemptions or those available under applicable state law. This is an "either/or" choice—debtors are not allowed to choose to use some state exemptions and some federal exemptions. When a petition is filed jointly by husband and wife or where the individual cases of a husband and wife are ordered to be jointly administered, each spouse must choose the same set of exemptions.[3] However, debtors in many states have no choice to make because their state law prohibits the use of the federal exemptions.[4] These federal exemptions are available to debtors *only* to the extent they are not prohibited by the applicable state.[5] Nonetheless, while the homestead exemption in many states is greater than the federal homestead exemption, provisions were introduced in BAPCPA that impose limitations on the extent to which debtors can avail themselves of a state's homestead exemption.

BAPCPA's Effect on Homestead Exemptions

BAPCPA established a maximum homestead exemption[6] for all debtors in all states unless a minimum period for property ownership was met. Subsection 522(p) of the Bankruptcy Code[7] generally prohibits exempting an equity interest in the property that was acquired by the debtor during the 1215-day period immediately preceding the bankruptcy filing to the extent that the interest exceeds $146,450 in value.[8] This limit may also apply in some cases in which the debtor has been convicted of a felony[9] or has a debt resulting from violations of securities laws, fraud in a fiduciary capacity, or as the result of certain acts that caused serious physical injury or death.[10] Additionally, if any part of the debtor's value in the residence is attributable to property disposed of in the 10-year period preceding the bankruptcy, the debtor's value in the residence must be reduced if all or part of the value in the previously owned property could not have been exempted in bankruptcy if the property were still owned when the debtor filed for bankruptcy.[11]

BAPCPA also restricts debtors' options for determining their domiciliary state, which may effectively place limits on their homestead exemption. Debtors must have lived in their current state for at least two years before they are eligible for that state's exemptions. Debtors who have not lived in the same state for at least two years[12] prior to filing for bankruptcy must look back at where they lived for the 180-day period immediately preceding that two years. If the debtor lived in more than one state during that 180-day period, the domiciliary state is the one in which the debtor lived for the greater part of that 180-day period.

Thus, through the changes made to § 522, BAPCPA limits the extent to which a debtor might plan for bankruptcy and maximize exempt assets. To effectively choose which state's exemptions will apply, a debtor must move to the chosen state approximately two years before filing for bankruptcy. To plan for a homestead exemption of more than $146,450, the debtor must acquire the interest approximately three years and four months before filing a bankruptcy petition.

Table 1. State Homestead Exemptions

State	Description of Property and Amount	Applicability of Federal Exemptions
Alabama	Homestead: $5,000 **Ala. Code § 6-10-2 (2011). Homestead exemption generally** The homestead of every resident of this state, with the improvements and appurtenances, not exceeding in value $5,000 and in area 160 acres, shall be, to the extent of any interest he or she may have therein, whether a fee or less estate or whether held in common or in severalty, exempt from levy and sale under execution or other process for the collection of debts during his or her life and occupancy and, if he or she leaves surviving him or her a spouse and a minor child, or children, or either, during the life of the surviving spouse and minority of the child, or children, but the area of the homestead shall not be enlarged by reason of any encumbrance thereon or of the character of the estate or interest owned therein by him or her. When a husband and wife jointly own a homestead each is entitled to claim separately the exemption provided herein, to the same extent and value as an unmarried individual. For purposes of this section and Sections 6- 10-38 and 6-10-40, a mobile home or similar dwelling if the principal place of residence of the individual claiming the exemption shall be deemed to be a homestead.	Federal exemptions *not* permitted. **Ala. Code § 6-10-11 (2011).** **Bankruptcy; Title 11 cases** In cases instituted under the provisions of Title 11 of the United States Code entitled "Bankruptcy," there shall be exempt from the property of the estate of an individual debtor only that property and income which is exempt under the laws of the State of Alabama and under federal laws other than Subsection (d) of Section 522 of said Title 11 of the United States Code.

Table 1. (Continued)

State	Description of Property and Amount	Applicability of Federal Exemptions
Alaska	Homestead: $70,200 **Alaska Stat. § 09.38.010 (2011). Homestead exemption** (a) An individual is entitled to an exemption as a homestead of the individual's interest in property in this state used as the principal residence of the individual or the dependents of the individual, but the value of the homestead exemption may not exceed $54,000. (b) If property owned by the entirety or in common is used by one or more individual owners or their dependents as their principal residence, each owner is entitled to a homestead exemption of that owner's interest in the property as provided in (a) of this section. The aggregate value of multiple homestead exemptions allowable with respect to a single living unit may not exceed $54,000. If there are multiple owners of property exempt as a homestead, the value of the exemption of each individual owner may not exceed the individual owner's pro rata portion of $54,000. **Alaska Admin. Code tit. 8, § 95.030 (2011). Adjusted exemption amounts** (a) Notwithstanding the amount provided for a homestead exemption under AS 09.38.010(a) and (b), the amount of the homestead exemption under AS 09.38.010(a) and (b) is $70,200.	Use of federal exemptions are permitted.[a]

State	Description of Property and Amount	Applicability of Federal Exemptions
Arizona	Homestead: $150,000 **Ariz. Rev. Stat. § 33-1101 (2011). Homestead exemptions; persons entitled to hold homesteads** A. Any person the age of eighteen or over, married or single, who resides within the state may hold as a homestead exempt from attachment, execution and forced sale, not exceeding one hundred fifty thousand dollars in value, any one of the following: 1. The person's interest in real property in one compact body upon which exists a dwelling house in which the person resides. 2. The person's interest in one condominium or cooperative in which the person resides. 3. A mobile home in which the person resides. 4. A mobile home in which the person resides plus the land upon which that mobile home is located.	Federal exemptions *not* permitted. **Ariz. Rev. Stat. § 33-1133 (2011). Other exemption laws** A. Nothing in this article shall be construed to displace other provisions of law which afford additional or greater protection to a debtor's property. B. Notwithstanding subsection A, in accordance with 11 U.S.C. 522(b), residents of this state are not entitled to the federal exemptions provided in 11 U.S.C. 522(d). Nothing in this section affects the exemptions provided to residents of this state by the constitution or statutes of this state.
Arkansas	Homestead: $2,500 + $800 if unmarried or $1,250 if married **Ark. Code Ann. § 16-66-210 (2011). Homestead Exemption Act** (b) The homestead of any resident of this state who is married or the head of a family shall not be subject to the lien of any judgment, or decree of any court, or to sale under execution or other process thereon, except such as may be rendered for the purchase money or for specific liens, laborers' or mechanics' liens for improving the	Residents may elect federal or state exemptions. **Ark. Code Ann. § 16-66-217 (2011). Election of bankruptcy exemptions** Residents of this state having the right to claim exemptions in a bankruptcy proceeding pursuant to 11 U.S.C. § 522 shall have the right to elect either:

Table 1. (Continued)

State	Description of Property and Amount	Applicability of Federal Exemptions
	homestead, or for taxes, or against executors,administrators, guardians, receivers, attorneys for moneys collected by them, and other trustees of an express trust for moneys due from them, in their fiduciary capacity. (c) (1) The homestead outside any city, town, or village, owned and occupied as a residence, shall consist of no more than one hundred sixty (160) acres of land, with the improvements thereon, to be selected by the owner. The homestead shall not exceed in value the sum of two thousand five hundred dollars ($2,500), but, in no event shall the homestead be reduced to less than eighty (80) acres, without regard to value. (2) The homestead in any city, town, or village, owned and occupied as a residence, shall consist of not more than one (1) acre of land, with the improvements thereon, to be selected by the owner. The homestead shall not exceed the sum of two thousand five hundred dollars ($2,500) in value, but in no event shall the homestead be reduced to less than one-quarter (1/4) of an acre of land, without regard to value. (3) Any homestead outside any city, town, or village, owned and occupied as a residence, which is annexed to or made part of an incorporated city or town within the State of Arkansas, shall retain its exemption under subdivision (c)(1) of this section as long as the land on	(i) The property exemptions provided by the Constitution and the laws of the State of Arkansas; or (ii) The property exemptions provided by 11 U.S.C. § 522(d).

State	Description of Property and Amount	Applicability of Federal Exemptions
	which it is located remains rural in nature and has a significant agricultural use. (d) The homestead provided for in this section shall inure to the benefit of the minor children, under the exemptions provided in this section, after the demise of the parents. **Ark. Code Ann. § 16-66-218 (2011). Exemptions from execution under federal bankruptcy proceedings** (a) The following property shall be exempt from execution under bankruptcy proceedings pursuant to P.L.95-598: (1) The unmarried debtor's aggregate interest, not exceeding eight hundred dollars ($800) in value, and the married debtor's aggregate interest, not exceeding one thousand two hundred fifty dollars ($1,250) in value, in real or personal property that the debtor or a dependent of the debtor uses as a residence, in a cooperative that owns property that the debtor or a dependent of the debtor uses as a residence, or in a burial plot for the debtor or a dependent of the debtor.	
California	Homestead: $75,000-$175,000 depending on facts and circumstances. See statute. **Cal. Civ. Proc. Code § 704.710 (2011). Definitions** As used in this article: (c) "Homestead" means the principal dwelling (1) in which the judgment debtor or the judgment debtor's spouse resided on the date the judgment creditor's lien attached to	Federal exemptions *not* permitted. **Cal. Civ. Proc. Code § 703.130 (2011). Exemptions in bankruptcy** Pursuant to the authority of paragraph (1) of subsection (b) of Section 522 of Title 11 of the United States Code, the exemptions set forth in subsection (d) of Section 522 of

Table 1. (Continued)

State	Description of Property and Amount	Applicability of Federal Exemptions
	the dwelling, and (2) in which the judgment debtor or the judgment debtor's spouse resided continuou-sly thereafter until the date of the court determination that the dwelling is a homestead. Where exempt proceeds from the sale or damage or destruction of a homestead are used toward the acquisition of a dwelling within the six-month period provided by Section 704.720, "homestead" also means the dwelling so acquired if it is the principal dwelling in which the judgment debtor or the judgment debtor's spouse resided continuously from the date of acquisition until the date of the court determination that the dwelling is a homestead, whether or not an abstract or certified copy of a judgment was recorded to create a judgment lien before the dwelling was acquired. … **Cal. Civ. Proc. Code § 704.730 (2011). Amount of homestead exemption** (a) The amount of the homestead exemption is one of the following: (1) Seventy-five thousand dollars ($75,000) unless the judgment debtor or spouse of the judgment debtor who resides in the homestead is a person described in paragraph (2) or (3). (2) One hundred thousand dollars ($100,000) if the judgment debtor or spouse of the judgment debtor who resides in the homestead is at the time of the attempted	Title 11 of the United States Code (Bankruptcy) are not authorized in this state.

State	Description of Property and Amount	Applicability of Federal Exemptions
	sale of the homestead a member of a family unit, and there is at least one member of the family unit who owns no interest in the homestead or whose only interest in the homestead is a community property interest with the judgment debtor. (3) One hundred seventy-five thousand dollars ($175,000) if the judgment debtor or spouse of the judgment debtor who resides in the homestead is at the time of the attempted sale of the homestead any one of the following: (A) A person 65 years of age or older. (B) A person physically or mentally disabled who as a result of that disability is unable to engage in substantial gainful employment. There is a rebuttable presumption affecting the burden of proof that a person receiving disability insurance benefit payments under Title II or supplemental security income payments under Title XVI of the federal Social Security Act satisfies the requirements of this paragraph as to his or her inability to engage in substantial gainful employment. (C) A person 55 years of age or older with a gross annual income of not more than fifteen thousand dollars ($15,000) or, if the judgment debtor is married, a gross annual income, including the gross annual income of the judgment debtor's spouse, of not more than twenty thousand dollars ($20,000) and the sale is an involuntary sale.	

Table 1. (Continued)

State	Description of Property and Amount	Applicability of Federal Exemptions
	(b) Notwithstanding any other provision of this section, the combined homestead exemptions of spouses on the same judgment shall not exceed the amount specified in paragraph (2) or (3), whichever is applicable, of subdivision (a), regardless of whether the spouses are jointly obligated on the judgment and regardless of whether the homestead consists of community or separate property or both. Notwithstanding any other provision of this article, if both spouses are entitled to a homestead exemption, the exemption of proceeds of the homestead shall be apportioned between the spouses on the basis of their proportionate interests in the homestead. ***See also*: Cal. Civ. Proc. Code § 703.140 (2011).** **Election of exemptions if bankruptcy petition is filed** (a) In a case under Title 11 of the United States Code, all of the exemptions provided by this chapter, including the homestead exemption, other than the provisions of subdivision (b) are applicable regardless of whether there is a money judgment against the debtor or whether a money judgment is being enforced by execution sale or any other procedure, but the exemptions provided by subdivision (b) may be elected in lieu of all other exemptions provided by this chapter, as follows: (1) If a husband and wife are joined in the petition, they jointly may elect to utilize the	

State	Description of Property and Amount	Applicability of Federal Exemptions
	applicable exemption provisions of this chapter other than the provisions of subdivision (b), or to utilize the applicable exemptions set forth in subdivision (b), but not both. (2) If the petition is filed individually, and not jointly, for a husband or a wife, the exemptions provided by this chapter other than the provisions of subdivision (b) are applicable, except that, if both the husband and the wife effectively waive in writing the right to claim, during the period the case commenced by filing the petition is pending, the exemptions provided by the applicable exemption provisions of this chapter, other than subdivision (b), in any case commenced by filing a petition for either of them under Title 11 of the United States Code, then they may elect to instead utilize the applicable exemptions set forth in subdivision (b). (3) If the petition is filed for an unmarried person, that person may elect to utilize the applicable exemption provisions of this chapter other than subdivision (b), or to utilize the applicable exemptions set forth in subdivision (b), but not both. (b) The following exemptions may be elected as provided in subdivision (a): (1) The debtor's aggregate interest, not to exceed seventeen thousand four hundred twenty-five dollars ($17,425) in value, in real property or personal property that the debtor or a dependent of the debtor uses as a	

Table 1. (Continued)

State	Description of Property and Amount	Applicability of Federal Exemptions
	residence, in a cooperative that owns property that the debtor or a dependent of the debtor uses as a residence, or in a burial plot for the debtor or a dependent of the debtor.	
Colorado	Homestead: $60,000-$90,000 depending on facts and circumstances. See statute. **Colo. Rev. Stat. § 38-41-201 (2010). Homestead exemption – definitions** (1) Every homestead in the state of Colorado shall be exempt from execution and attachment arising from any debt, contract, or civil obligation not exceeding in actual cash value in excess of any liens or encumbrances on the homesteaded property in existence at the time of any levy of execution thereon: (a) The sum of sixty thousand dollars if the homestead is occupied as a home by an owner thereof or an owner's family; or (b) The sum of ninety thousand dollars if the homestead is occupied as a home by an elderly or disabled owner, an elderly or disabled spouse of an owner, or an elderly or disabled dependent of an owner. **Colo. Rev. Stat. § 38-41-201.6 (2010). Mobile home, manufactured home, trailer, and trailer coach homestead exemption** (1) ... For purposes of this homestead exemption, the term "house" as used in section 38-41-205 shall be deemed to	**Federal exemptions *not* permitted.** **Colo. Rev. Stat. § 13-54-107 (2010). Exemptions in bankruptcy** The exemptions provided in section 522 (d) of the federal bankruptcy code of 1978, title 11 of the United States Code, as amended, are denied to residents of this state. Exemptions authorized to be claimed by residents of this state shall be limited to those exemptions expressly provided by the statutes of this state.

State	Description of Property and Amount	Applicability of Federal Exemptions
	include mobile homes or manufactured homes. (2) ... For purposes of this homestead exemption, the term "house" as used in section 38-41-205 shall be deemed to include trailers or trailer coaches.	
Connecticut	Homestead: $75,000-$125,000 depending on facts and circumstances. See statute. Wildcard: $1,000 **Conn. Gen. Stat. § 52-352b (2011). Exempt property** The following property of any natural person shall be exempt: (r) Any interest of the exemptioner in any property not to exceed in value one thousand dollars; (t) The homestead of the exemptioner to the value of seventy-five thousand dollars, or, in the case of a money judgment arising out of services provided at a hospital, to the value of one hundred twenty-five thousand dollars, provided value shall be determined as the fair market value of the real property less the amount of any statutory or consensual lien which encumbers it.	No statutory prohibition. Use of federal exemptions permitted.
Delaware	Homestead: $75,000 in 2010, $100,000 in 2011, and $125,000 in 2012, unless totally disabled or married and at least one of the spouses is at least 65 years old. See statute. **Del. Code Ann., tit. 10, § 4914 (2011). Exemptions in bankruptcy and insolvency**	Federal exemptions *not* permitted. **Del. Code Ann., tit. 10, § 4914 (2011). Exemptions in bankruptcy and insolvency** (a) In accordance with § 522(b) of the Bankruptcy Reform Act of 1978 (11 U.S.C. § 522(b)), in any bankruptcy proceeding,

Table 1. (Continued)

State	Description of Property and Amount	Applicability of Federal Exemptions
	(c) In any federal bankruptcy or state insolvency proceeding, an individual debtor and/or such individual's spouse domiciled in Delaware shall be authorized to exempt from the bankruptcy or insolvency estate … (1) Equity in real property or equity in a manufactured home (as defined in Chapter 70 of Title 25) which constitutes a [debtor's] principal residence in an aggregate amount not to exceed ...$75,000 in 2010, $100,000 in 2011, and $125,000 in 2010, except that the exemption for persons totally disabled from working or married persons where at least one of the spouses is 65 years old or older shall be $125,000 effective immediately… (d) This section shall apply separately with respect to each debtor in a joint case but not to exceed … $125,000 in value in a principal residence in an individual or a joint case...	an individual debtor domiciled in Delaware is not authorized or entitled to elect the federal exemptions as set forth in § 522(d) of the Bankruptcy Reform Act of 1978 (11 U.S.C. § 522(d)) and may exempt only that property from the estate as set forth in subsection (b) of this section.
District of Columbia	Homestead: Unlimited dollar amount **D.C. Code § 15-501 (2011). Exempt property of householder; property in transitu; debt for wages** (a) The following property of the head of a family or householder residing in the District of Columbia, or of a person who earns the major portion of his livelihood in the District of Columbia, being the head of a family or householder, regardless of his place of residence, is free and exempt from distraint, attachment, levy, or seizure and	No statutory prohibition. Use of federal exemptions permitted.

State	Description of Property and Amount	Applicability of Federal Exemptions
	sale on execution or decree of any court in the District of Columbia: (14) the debtor's aggregate interest in real property used as the residence of the debtor, or property that the debtor or a dependent of the debtor in a cooperative that owns property that the debtor or a dependent of the debtor uses as a residence, or in a burial plot for the debtor or dependent of the debtor, except nothing relative to these exemptions shall impair the following debt instruments on real property: deed of trust, mortgage, mechanic's lien, or tax lien.	
Florida	Homestead: Unlimited dollar amount **Fla. Const., Art. X § 4 (2011). Homestead; exemptions** (a) There shall be exempt from forced sale under process of any court, and no judgment, decree or execution shall be a lien thereon, except for the payment of taxes and assessments thereon, obligations contracted for the purchase, improvement or repair thereof, or obligations contracted for house, field or other labor performed on the realty, the following property owned by a natural person: (1) a homestead, if located outside a municipality, to the extent of one hundred sixty acres of contiguous land and improvements thereon, which shall not be reduced without the owner's consent by reason of subsequent inclusion in a municipality; or if located within a municipality, to the extent of one-half acre of contiguous land, upon which the	With the exception of 11 U.S.C. § 522(d)(10), federal exemptions *not* permitted. **Fla. Stat. § 222.20 (2011). Nonavailability of federal bankruptcy exemptions** In accordance with the provision of s. 522(b) of the Bankruptcy Code of 1978 (11 U.S.C. s. 522(b)), residents of this state shall not be entitled to the federal exemptions provided in s. 522(d) of the Bankruptcy Code of 1978 (11 U.S.C. s. 522(d)). Nothing herein shall affect the exemptions given to residents of this state by the State Constitution and the Florida Statutes. **Fla. Stat. § 222.201 (2011). Availability of federal bankruptcy exemptions** (1) Notwithstanding § 222.20, an individual

Table 1. (Continued)

State	Description of Property and Amount	Applicability of Federal Exemptions
	exemption shall be limited to the residence of the owner or the owner's family. **Fla. Stat. § 222.05 (2011). Setting apart leasehold** Any person owning and occupying any dwelling house, including a mobile home used as a residence, or modular home, on land not his or her own which he or she may lawfully possess, by lease or otherwise, and claiming such house, mobile home, or modular home as his or her homestead, shall be entitled to the exemption of such house, mobile home, or modular home from levy and sale as aforesaid.	debtor under the federal Bankruptcy Reform Act of 1978 may exempt, in addition to any other exemptions allowed under state law, any property listed in subsection (d)(10) of s. 522 of that act.
Georgia	Homestead: $10,000; $20,000 if joint (may be used for a burial plot as well as a residence) Wildcard: $600 **Ga. Code Ann. § 44-13-1 (2011). Amount of exemption; who may claim exemption; what charges enforceable** Except as otherwise provided in this article, there shall be exempt from levy and sale by virtue of any process whatever under the laws of this state any real or personal property or both of a debtor in the amount of $5,000.00. No court or ministerial officer in this state shall ever have jurisdiction or authority to enforce any judgment, execution, or decree against property set apart under this Code section, including such improvements as may be made thereon from time to time, except for taxes, for the	Federal exemptions *not* permitted. **Ga. Code Ann. § 44-13-100 (2011). Amount of exemption; who may claim exemption; what charges enforceable** (b) Pursuant to 11 U.S.C. Section 522(b)(1), an individual debtor whose domicile is in Georgia is prohibited from applying or utilizing 11 U.S.C. Section 522(d) in connection with exempting property from his or her estate; and such individual debtor may exempt from property of his or her estate only such property as may be exempted from the estate pursuant to 11 U.S.C. Section 522(b)(2)(A) and (B).

State	Description of Property and Amount	Applicability of Federal Exemptions
	purchase money of the property, for labor done on the property, for material furnished for the property, or for the removal of encumbrances on the property. **Ga. Code Ann. § 44-13-100 (2011). Exemptions for purposes of bankruptcy and intestate insolvent estates** (a) In lieu of the exemption provided in Code Section 44-13-1, any debtor who is a natural person may exempt, pursuant to this article, for purposes of bankruptcy, the following property: (1) The debtor's aggregate interest, not to exceed $10,000.00 in value, in real property or personal property that the debtor or a dependent of the debtor uses as a residence, in a cooperative that owns property that the debtor or a dependent of the debtor uses as a residence, or in a burial plot for the debtor or a dependent of the debtor. In the event title to property used for the exemption provided under this paragrap h is in one of two spouses who is a debtor, the amount of the exemption hereunder shall be $20,000.00; (6) The debtor's aggregate interest, not to exceed $600.00 in value plus any unused amount of the exemption, not to exceed $5,000.00, provided under paragraph (1) of this subsection, in any property.	For the purposes of this subsection, an 'individual debtor whose domicile is in Georgia' means an individual whose domicile has been located in Georgia for the 180 days immediately preceding the date of the filing of the bankruptcy petition or for a longer portion of such 180 day period than in any other place.

Table 1. (Continued)

State	Description of Property and Amount	Applicability of Federal Exemptions
Hawaii	Homestead: $20,000-$30,000 depending on facts and circumstances. See statute. **Haw. Rev. Stat. § 651-91 (2011). Definitions** As used in this subpart: (5) “Real property” consists of the dwelling house in which the owner resides and one parcel of land not to exceed one acre, upon which it is situated together with other buildings thereon. This parcel may be in fee simple or any other interest in real property which vests the immediate right of possession, even though such right of possession is not exclusive, and includes land held under long-term lease, ownership rights in a condominium or stock cooperative unit. **Haw. Rev. Stat. § 651-92 (2011). Real property exempt** (a) Real property shall be exempt from attachment or execution as follows: (1) An interest in one parcel of real property in the State of Hawaii of a fair market value not exceeding $30,000 owned by the defendant who is either the head of a family or an individual sixty-five years of age or older. (2) An interest in one parcel of real property in the State of Hawaii of a fair market value not exceeding $20,000 owned by the defendant who is a person. The fair market value of the interest exempted in	No statutory prohibition. Use of federal exemptions permitted.

State	Description of Property and Amount	Applicability of Federal Exemptions
	paragraphs (1) or (2) shall be determined by appraisal and shall be an interest which is over and above all liens and encumbrances on the real property recorded prior to the lien under which attachment or execution is to be made. Not more than one exemption shall be claimed on any one parcel of real property even though more than one person residing on such real property may otherwise be entitled to an exemption. **Haw. Rev. Stat. § 651-93 (2011). Effect of separation, divorce, reconciliation** Following the entry of a decree of separate maintenance or an interlocutory decree of divorce, each spouse may claim a separate real property exemption under this part as a person. A subsequent reconciliation of the spouses when evidenced by a dismissal of the divorce action or vacation of the decree of separate maintenance executed by both spouses or their attorneys of record shall cancel a separate claim for a real property exemption and the spouses shall only have one real property exemption.	
Idaho	Homestead: $100,000 **Idaho Code Ann. § 55-1001 (2011). Definitions** For purposes of this chapter: (1) "Dwelling house" and "mobile home" include manufactured housing. (2) "Homestead" means and consists of the dwelling house or the mobile home in which the owner resides or	Federal exemptions *not* permitted. **Idaho Code Ann. § 11-609 (2011). Nonauthorization of federal bankruptcy exemptions** In any federal bankruptcy proceeding, an individual debtor may exempt from property of the estate only such property as

Table 1. (Continued)

State	Description of Property and Amount	Applicability of Federal Exemptions
	intends to reside, with appurtenant buildings, and the land on which the same are situated and by which the same are surrounded, or improved; or unimproved land owned with the intention of placing a house or mobile home thereon and residing thereon. A mobile home may be exempted under this chapter whether or not it is permanently affixed to the underlying land and whether or not the mobile home is placed upon a lot owned by the mobile home owner. Property included in the homestead must be actually intended or used as a principal home for the owner. (3) "Net value" means market value less all liens and encumbrances. (4) "Owner" includes, but is not limited to, a purchaser under a deed of trust, mortgage, or contract, or a person who takes the subject property under a life estate. **Idaho Code Ann. § 55-1003 (2011). Homestead exemption limited** A homestead may consist of lands, as described in section 55-1001, Idaho Code, regardless of area, but the homestead exemption amount shall not exceed the lesser of (i) the total net value of the lands, mobile home, and improvements as described in section 55-1001, Idaho Code; or (ii) the sum of one hundred thousand dollars ($100,000).	is specified under the laws of this state.

State	Description of Property and Amount	Applicability of Federal Exemptions
Illinois	Homestead: $15,000; if property is owned by two or more persons, each may exempt proportionate share of $30,000. **735 Ill. Comp. Stat. 5/12-901 (2011). Amount** Every individual is entitled to an estate of homestead to the extent in value of $15,000 of his or her interest in a farm or lot of land and buildings thereon, a condominium, or personal property, owned or rightly possessed by lease or otherwise and occupied by him or her as a residence, or in a cooperative that owns property that the individual uses as a residence. That homestead and all right in and title to that homestead is exempt from attachment, judgment, levy, or judgment sale for the payment of his or her debts or other purposes and from the laws of conveyance, descent, and legacy, except as provided in this Code or in Section 20-6 of the Probate Act of 1975 [755 ILCS 5/20-6]. This Section is not applicable between joint tenants or tenants in common but it is applicable as to any creditors of those persons. If 2 or more individuals own property that is exempt as a homestead, the value of the exemption of each individual may not exceed his or her proportionate share of $30,000 based upon percentage of ownership.	Federal exemptions *not* permitted. **735 Ill. Comp. Stat. 5/12-1201 (2011). Bankruptcy exemption** In accordance with the provision of Section 522(b) of the Bankruptcy Code of 1978, (11 U.S.C. 522(b)), residents of this State shall be prohibited from using the federal exemptions provided in Section 522(d) of the Bankruptcy Code of 1978 (11 U.S.C. 522(d)), except as may otherwise be permitted under the laws of Illinois.
Indiana	Homestead: $15,000; $15,000 each available to joint debtors for property held as tenants by the entireties. **Ind. Code Ann. § 34-55-10-2 (2011). Amount of exemption** (c) The following property of a debtor domiciled in Indiana is exempt:	Federal exemptions *not* permitted. **Ind. Code Ann. § 34-55-10-1 (2011). Exemptions prohibited and allowed** In accordance with Section 522(b) of the Bankruptcy Code of 1978 (11 U.S.C.S.

Table 1. (Continued)

State	Description of Property and Amount	Applicability of Federal Exemptions
	(1) Real estate or personal property constituting the personal or family residence of the debtor or a dependent of the debtor, or estates or rights in that real estate or personal property, of not more than fifteen thousand dollars ($15,000). The exemption under this subdivision is individually available to joint debtors concerning property held by them as tenants by the entireties. (2) Other real estate or tangible personal property of eight thousand dollars ($8,000). (5) Any interest that the debtor has in real estate held as a tenant by the entireties. The exemption under this subdivision does not apply to a debt for which the debtor and the debtor's spouse are jointly liable.	522(b)), in any bankruptcy proceeding, an individual debtor domiciled in Indiana is not entitled to the federal exemptions as provided by Section 522(d) of the Bankruptcy Code of 1978 (11 U.S.C.S. 522(d)).
Iowa	Homestead: Unlimited dollar amount **Iowa Code § 561.1 (2011). "Homestead" defined** 1. The homestead must embrace the house used as a home by the owner, and, if the owner has two or more houses thus used, the owner may select which the owner will retain. It may contain one or more contiguous lots or tracts of land, with the building and other appurtenances thereon, habitually and in good faith used as part of the same homestead. **Iowa Code § 561.2 (2011). Extent and value** If within a city plat, it must not exceed one-half acre in extent, otherwise it must not contain in the aggregate	Federal exemptions *not* permitted. **Iowa Code § 627.10 (2011). Bankruptcy exemption** A debtor to whom the law of this state applies on the date of filing of a petition in bankruptcy is not entitled to elect to exempt from property of the bankruptcy estate the property that is specified in 11 U.S.C. § 522(d) (1979). This section is enacted for the purpose set forth in 11 U.S.C. § 522(b)(1) (1979).

State	Description of Property and Amount	Applicability of Federal Exemptions
	more than forty acres, but if, in either case, its value is less than five hundred dollars, it may be enlarged until it reaches that amount.	
Kansas	Homestead: Unlimited dollar amount **Kan. Stat. Ann. § 60-2301 (2011). Homestead; extent of exemption** A homestead to the extent of 160 acres of farming land, or of one acre within the limits of an incorporated town or city, or a manufactured home or mobile home, occupied as a residence by the owner or by the family of the owner, or by both the owner and family thereof, together with all the improvements on the same, shall be exempted from forced sale under any process of law, and shall not be alienated without the joint consent of husband and wife, when that relation exists; but no property shall be exempt from sale for taxes, or for the payment of obligations contracted for the purchase of said premises, or for the erection of improvements thereon. The provisions of this section shall not apply to any process of law obtained by virtue of a lien given by the consent of both husband and wife, when that relation exists.	With the exception of 11 U.S.C. §522(d)(10), federal exemptions *not* permitted. **Kan. Stat. Ann. § 60-2312 (2011). No right to elect exemptions under federal law, exception** (a) Except as provided in subsection (b), no person, as an individual debtor under the federal bankruptcy reform act of 1978 (11 U.S.C. 101 et seq.), may elect exemptions pursuant to subsection (b)(1) of section 522 of such federal act. (b) An individual debtor under the federal bankruptcy reform act of 1978 may exempt, in addition to any other exemptions allowed under state law, any property listed in subsection (d)(10) of section 522 of such federal act. The provisions of this subsection shall apply to any bankruptcy action which: (1) Is filed on or after July 1, 1986; or (2) was filed on or after April 26, 1980, and is pending or on appeal on July 1, 1986.
Kentucky	Homestead: $5,000 unless debt predates purchase or improvement of property Wildcard: $1,000	Debtors domiciled in Kentucky may elect federal or state exemption \

Table 1. (Continued)

State	Description of Property and Amount	Applicability of Federal Exemptions
	Ky. Rev. Stat. Ann. § 427.060 (2011). Homestead and burial plot exemptions—Exceptions In addition to any exemption of personal property, an individual debtor's aggregate interest, not to exceed five thousand dollars ($5,000) in value, in real or personal property that such debtor or a dependent of such debtor uses as a permanent residence in this state, or in a burial plot for such debtor or a dependent of such debtor is exempt from sale under execution, attachment or judgment, except to foreclose a mortgage given by the owner of a homestead or for purchase money due thereon. This exemption shall not apply if the debt or liability existed prior to the purchase of the property or the erection of the improvements thereon. **Ky. Rev. Stat. Ann. § 427.160 (2011). Additional general exemption** Solely for the purpose of applying the provisions of 11 U.S.C. sec. 522(b)(3)(A) in a federal bankruptcy proceeding, in addition to other exemptions provided in this chapter and only to the extent otherwise allowed by applicable federal law, every debtor shall have a general exemption not to exceed one thousand dollars ($1,000) in value to be applied toward any property, real or personal, tangible or intangible in his estate when he or she has filed for bankruptcy under the provisions of The Bankruptcy	**Ky. Rev. Stat. Ann. § 427.170 (2011). Federal bankruptcy code exemptions applicable in Kentucky** Solely for the purpose of applying the provisions of 11 U.S.C. sec. 522(b)(2) in a federal bankruptcy proceeding and only to the extent otherwise allowed by applicable federal law, an individual debtor domiciled in this state is authorized to exempt from property of said debtor's bankruptcy estate the property specified under 11 U.S.C. sec. 522(d).

State	Description of Property and Amount	Applicability of Federal Exemptions
	Code of 1978, 92 Stat. 2549 (1978), P.L. 95- 598, as amended.	
Louisiana	Homestead; $35,000 – Unlimited depending on facts and circumstances. See statute. **La. Const. Art. XII, § 9 (2011). Exemptions from seizure and sale** The legislature shall provide by law for exemptions from seizure and sale, as well as waivers of and exclusions from such exemptions. The exemption shall extend to at least fifteen thousand dollars in value of a homestead, as provided by law. **La. Rev. Stat. § 20:1 (2011). Declaration of homestead; exemption from seizure and sale; debts excluded from exemption; waiver; certain proceeds from property insurance exempted** A. (1) The bona fide homestead consists of a residence occupied by the owner and the land on which the residence is located, including any building and appurtenances located thereon, and any contiguous tracts up to a total of five acres if the residence is within a municipality, or up to a total of two hundred acres of land if the residence is not located in a municipality. (2) The homestead is exempt from seizure and sale under any writ, mandate, or process whatsoever, except as provided by Subsections C and D of this Section. This exemption extends to thirty-five thousand dollars in value of the homestead, except in the case of	Federal exemptions *not* permitted. **La. Rev. Stat. § 13:3881 (2011). General exemptions from seizure** B. (1) In cases instituted under the provisions of Title 11 of the United States Code, entitled "Bankruptcy," there shall be exempt from the property of the estate of an individual debtor only that property and income which is exempt under the laws of the state of Louisiana and under federal laws other than Subsection (d) of Section 522 of said Title 11 of the United States Code.

Table 1. (Continued)

State	Description of Property and Amount	Applicability of Federal Exemptions
	obligations arising directly as a result of a catastrophic or terminal illness or injury, in which case the exemption shall apply to the full value of the homestead based upon its value one year before such seizure. This homestead exemption from seizure and sale shall extend automatically to the proceeds from any property insurance policy received as a result of damage caused by a gubernatorially declared disaster to a homestead and that are held separately in an escrow account identified as insurance proceeds paid from the damage of a homestead for its repair or replacement. (3) For the purposes of this Section, "catastrophic or terminal illness or injury" shall mean an illness or injury which creates uninsured obligations to health care providers of more than ten thousand dollars and which are greater than fifty percent of the annual adjusted gross income of the debtor, as established by an average of federal income tax returns for the three preceding years.	
Maine	Homestead: $47,500-$95,000 depending on facts and circumstances. See statute. Wildcard: $400 **Me. Rev. Stat. Ann. tit. 14, § 4422 (2011). Exempt Property** The following property is exempt from attachment and execution, except to the extent that it has been fraudulently conveyed by the debtor.	Federal exemptions *not* permitted. **Me. Rev. Stat. Ann. tit. 14, § 4426 (2011). Exemptions in bankruptcy proceedings** Notwithstanding anything to the contrary in the United States Code, Title 11, Section 522(b), a debtor may exempt from property of the debtor's estate under United States Code, Title 11, only that property exempt

State	Description of Property and Amount	Applicability of Federal Exemptions
	1. RESIDENCE. The exemption of a debtor's residence is subject to this subsection. A. Except as provided in paragraph B, the debtor's aggregate interest, not to exceed $47,500 in value, in real or personal property that the debtor or a dependent of the debtor uses as a residence, in a cooperative that owns property that the debtor or a dependent of the debtor uses as a residence, or in a burial plot for the debtor or a dependent of the debtor, except that if minor dependents of the debtor have their principal place of residence with the debtor, the debtor's aggregate interest may not exceed $95,000 and except that if the debtor's interest is held jointly with any other person or persons, the exemption may not exceed in value the lesser of $47,500 or the product of the debtor's fractional share times $95,000. B. The debtor's aggregate interest, not to exceed $95,000 in value, in property described in paragraph A, if the debtor or a dependent of the debtor is either a person 60 years of age or older or a person physically or mentally disabled and because of such disability is unable to engage in substantial gainful employment and whose disability has lasted or can be expected to last for at least 12 months or can be expected to result in death; except that if the debtor's interest is held jointly with any other person or persons, the exemption may not exceed in value the lesser of $95,000 or the product of the	under the United States Code, Title 11, Section 522(b)(2)(A) and (B),[b] except that any debtor eligible for a residence exemption under section 4422, subsection 1, paragraph B, may exempt the amount allowed in that paragraph.

Table 1. (Continued)

State	Description of Property and Amount	Applicability of Federal Exemptions
	fractional share of the debtor's interest times $190,000. This paragraph does not apply to liens obtained prior to its effective date or to judgments based on torts involving other than ordinary negligence on the part of the debtor. 15. OTHER PROPERTY. The debtor's aggregate interest, not to exceed in value $400, in any property, whether or not otherwise exempt under this section. 16. UNUSED RESIDENCE EXEMPTION. The debtor's interest, equal to any unused amount of the exemption provided under subsection 1 but not exceeding $6,000, in any property exempt under subsections 3 and 5 and subsection 14, paragraph D.	
Maryland	For cases filed before October 1, 2010: No specific homestead exemption Wildcard: $6,000, subject to time constraints, plus $5,000 in a bankruptcy proceeding for domiciliaries See statute. For cases filed after September 30, 2010: Homestead exemption equal to the amount provided in 11 U.S.C. § 522(d)(1) as adjusted in accordance with 11 U.S.C. § 104— currently $20,200; Wildcard: $6,000 subject to time constraints See Maryland S.B. 782 and H.B 456 **Md. Code Ann., Cts. & Jud. Proc. § 11-504 (2009).**	Federal exemptions *not* permitted. **Md. Code Ann., Cts. & Jud. Proc. § 11-504 (2011). Exemptions from execution** (g) Federal bankruptcy exemptions.—In any bankruptcy proceeding, a debtor is not entitled to the federal exemptions provided by § 522(d) of the federal Bankruptcy Code.

State	Description of Property and Amount	Applicability of Federal Exemptions
	Exemptions from execution [Effective for cases filed before October 1, 2010] (b) In general.—The following items are exempt from execution on a judgment: (5) Cash or property of any kind equivalent in value to $6,000 is exempt, if within 30 days from the date of the attachment or the levy by the sheriff, the debtor elects to exempt cash or selected items of property in an amount not to exceed a cumulative value of $6,000. (f) Interest in real or personal property.—In addition to the exemptions provided in subsection (b) of this section, and in other statutes of this State, in any proceeding under Title 11 of the United States Code, entitled "Bankruptcy," any individual debtor domiciled in this State may exempt the debtor's aggregate interest, not to exceed $5,000 in value, in real property or personal property. **Md. Code Ann., Cts. & Jud. Proc. § 11-504 (2011). Exemptions from execution [Effective for cases filed after September 30, 2010]** (b) In general.—The following items are exempt from execution on a judgment: (5) Cash or property of any kind equivalent in value to $6,000 is exempt, if within 30 days from the date of the attachment or the levy by the sheriff, the debtor elects to exempt cash or selected items of property in an amount not to exceed a cumulative value of $6,000.	

Table 1. (Continued)

State	Description of Property and Amount	Applicability of Federal Exemptions
	(f) Interest in real or personal property. – (1) In addition to the exemptions provided in subsection (b) of this section, and in other statutes of this State, in any proceeding under Title 11 of the United States Code, entitled "Bankruptcy," any individual debtor domiciled in this State may exempt the debtor's aggregate interest in: (i) Personal Property, up to $5,000; and (ii) Owner-occupied residential real property, up to the amount under 11 U.S.C. § 522(d)(1), adjusted in accordance with 11 U.S.C. § 104 subject to the provisions of paragraphs (2) and (3) of this subsection. (2) An individual may not claim the exemption under paragraph 1(ii) of this subsection on a particular property if: (i) The individual has claimed successfully the exemption on the property within 8 years prior to the filing of the bankruptcy proceeding in which the exemption under this subsection is claimed; or (ii) The individual's spouse, child, child's spouse, parent, sibling, grandparent, or grandchild has claimed successfully the exemption on the property within 8 years prior to the filing of the bankruptcy proceeding in which the exemption under this subsection is claimed. (3) The exemption under paragraph 1(ii) of this subsection may not be claimed by both a husband and wife in the same bankruptcy proceeding.	

State	Description of Property and Amount	Applicability of Federal Exemptions
Massachusetts	Homestead; $500,000; if elderly or disabled, $500,000 for each eligible individual who has an ownership interest in the property. [Effective through March 15, 2011 and for all estates of homestead in effect on March 16, 2011[c]] Automatic Homestead: $125,000 [Effective March 16, 2011] Declared Homestead: $500,000 [Effective March 16, 2011] **Mass. Gen. Laws ch. 188, § 1 (2011). Nature of Homestead Estate; Exceptions; "Owner" and "Family" Defined [Effective through March 15, 2011]** An estate of homestead to the extent of $500,000 in the land and buildings may be acquired pursuant to this chapter by an owner or owners of a home or one or all who rightfully possess the premise by lease or otherwise and who occupy or intend to occupy said home as a principal residence. Said estate shall be exempt from the laws of conveyance, descent, devise, attachment, levy on execution and sale for payment of debts or legacies except in the following cases: (1) sale for taxes; (2) for a debt contracted prior to the acquisition of said estate of homestead; (3) for a debt contracted for the purchase of said home; (4) upon an execution issued from the probate court to enforce its judgment that a spouse pay a certain amount	No statutory prohibition. Use of federal exemptions permitted.

Table 1. (Continued)

State	Description of Property and Amount	Applicability of Federal Exemptions
	weekly or otherwise for the support of a spouse or minor children; (5) where buildings on land not owned by the owner of a homestead estate are attached, levied upon or sold for the ground rent of the lot whereon they stand; (6) upon an execution issued from a court of competent jurisdiction to enforce its judgment based upon fraud, mistake, duress, undue influence or lack of capacity. For purposes of this chapter, an owner of a home shall include a sole owner, joint tenant, tenant by the entirety or tenant in common; provided, that only one owner may acquire an estate in a homestead in any such home for the benefit of his family; and provided further, that an estate of homestead may be acquired on only one principal residence for the benefit of a family. For the purposes of this chapter, the word "family" shall include either a parent and child or children, a husband and wife and their children, if any, or a sole owner. **Mass. Gen. Laws ch. 188, § 1 (2011). Definitions [Effective on March 16, 2011]** For the purposes of this chapter, the following words shall have the following meanings unless the context clearly requires otherwise: "Automatic homestead exemption", an exemption in the amount of $125,000 pursuant to section 4; provided,	

State	Description of Property and Amount	Applicability of Federal Exemptions
	however, that: (1) with respect to a home owned as joint tenants or as tenants by the entirety, the automatic homestead exemption shall remain whole and unallocated between the owners, provided that the owners together shall not be entitled to an automatic homestead exemption in excess of $125,000; and (2) with respect to a home owned by multiple owners as tenants in common or as trust beneficiaries, the automatic homestead exemption shall be allocated among all owners in proportion to their respective ownership interests. "Declared homestead exemption", an exemption in the amount of $500,000 created by a written declaration, executed and recorded pursuant to section 5; provided, however, that: (1) with respect to a home owned by joint tenants or tenants by the entirety who are benefited by an estate of homestead declared pursuant to section 3, the declared homestead exemption shall remain whole and unallocated, provided that the owners together shall not be entitled to a declared homestead exemption in excess of $500 ,000; (2) if a home is owned by tenants in common or trust beneficiaries, the declared homestead exemption for each co-tenant and trust beneficiary who benefits by an estate of homestead declared pursuant to said section 3 shall be the product of: (i) $50 0,000; and (ii) the cotenant's or trust beneficiary's percentage ownership interest; (3) except as provided in clause (4), each person who owns a	

Table 1. (Continued)

State	Description of Property and Amount	Applicability of Federal Exemptions
	home and who is benefited by an estate of homestead declared pursuant to section 2 shall be entitled to the declared homestead exemption without reduction, proration or allocation among other owners of the home; and (4) separate estates of homestead may be declared pursuant to sections 2 and 3 on the same home, and in such event: (i) if the home is owned by tenants in common or trust beneficiaries, the declared homestead exemption for each co-tenant and trust beneficiary who benefits by an estate of homestead declared pursuant to section 3 shall be calculated in the manner provided in clause (2), and the declared homestead exemption for each co-tenant and trust beneficiary who benefits by an estate of homestead eclared pursuant to section 2 shall be calculated in the manner provided in clause (3); or (ii) if the home is owned by joint tenants or tenants by the entirety, the declared homestead exemption for the owners together shall be the sum of $500,000 multiplied by the number of declarations recorded pursuant to section 2, plus $250,000; provided, however, that the homestead exemption under this subclause shall remain whole and unallocated among the owners; and provided further, that no owner who declares a homestead, acting individually, shall be entitled to claim an exemption of more than $500,000; and (5) the calculation of the amount of homestead exemption available to an owner	

State	Description of Property and Amount	Applicability of Federal Exemptions
	shall not sever a joint tenancy or tenancy by the entirety. "Disabled person", an individual who has a medically-determinable, permanent physical or mental impairment that would meet the disability requirements for Supplemental Security Income under 42 U.S.C. 1382c(a)(3)(A) and 42 U.S.C. 1382c(a)(3)(C) as in effect at the time of recording. "Elderly person", an individual 62 years of age or older. "Family" or "family members", (1) married individuals, both of whom own a home, and any minor child; (2) a married individual who owns a home, a non-titled spouse of the married individual and any minor child; or (3) an unmarried individual who owns a home and any minor child. "Home", the aggregate of: (1) any of the following: (i) a single-family dwelling, including accessory structures appurtenant thereto and the land on which it is located; (ii) a 2 to 4-family dwelling, including accessory structures appurtenant thereto and the land on which it is located; (iii) a manufactured home as defined in section 32Q of chapter 140; (iv) a unit in a condominium, as those terms are defined in section 1 of chapter 183A, that is used for residential purposes; or (v) a residential cooperative housing unit established pursuant to chapters 156B, 157B, 180 or otherwise; (2) the sale proceeds as provided in clause (1) of subsection (a) of	

Table 1. (Continued)

State	Description of Property and Amount	Applicability of Federal Exemptions
	section 11; and (3) the proceeds of any policy of insurance insuring the home against fire or other casualty loss as provided in clause (2) of said subsection (a) of said section 11. "Minor child", a person aged 21 and under, who is the natural or adopted child of an owner or owner's spouse entitled to the benefits of this chapter, notwithstanding any law to the contrary. "Owner", a natural person who is a sole owner, joint tenant, tenant by the entirety, tenant in common, life estate holder or holder of a beneficial interest in a trust. "Principal residence", the home where an owner, and the owner's family if applicable, resides or intends to reside as the primary dwelling; provided, however, that no person shall hold concurrent rights in more than 1 principal residence. "Record", "recording" or "recorded", the act of recording in the registry of deeds or the registry district of the land court for the county or district wherein the home lies, except that with respect to a manufactured home located on registered land, recording in the registry of deeds shall be sufficient. **Mass. Gen. Laws ch. 188, § 1A (2011). Protection from Attachment, Seizure or Execution of Judgment of Realty of Certain Elderly and Disabled Persons; Prerequisites; Exceptions; Termination of Homestead**	

State	Description of Property and Amount	Applicability of Federal Exemptions
	[Repealed Effective March 16, 2011] The real property or manufactured home of persons sixty-two years of age or older, regardless of marital status, or of a disabled person, as herein defined, shall be protected against attachment, seizure or execution of judgment to the extent of $500,000; provided, however, that such person has filed an elderly or disabled person's declaration of homestead protection as provided in section two; and, provided further, that such person occupies or intends to occupy such real property or manufactured home as his principal residence. A disabled person's declaration of homestead protection shall be accompanied by either of the documents referred to in the second paragraph of this section. … Each individual having an ownership interest in the real property or manufactured homes which serves as that individual's principal residence and who qualifies under the provisions of this section shall, upon filing of an elderly or disabled person's declaration of homestead protection, be eligible for protection of such ownership interest up to a maximum amount of $500,000 per individual, regardless of whether such declaration is filed individually or jointly with another. **Mass. Gen. Laws ch. 188, § 2 (2011). Estate of Homestead – Elderly or Disabled Persons [Effective**	

Table 1. (Continued)

State	Description of Property and Amount	Applicability of Federal Exemptions
	March 16, 2011] (a) The estate of homestead of each owner who is an elderly or disabled person, regardless of marital status, shall be protected under this section against attachment, seizure, execution on judgment, levy and sale for payment of debts and legacies, except as provided in subsection (b) of section 3, to the extent of the declared homestead exemption; provided, however, that the declaration of homestead for such elderly or disabled person that complies with section 5 has been recorded; and provided, further, that each owner occupies or intends to occupy the home as his principal residence. An owner of a home who qualifies under this section shall, upon recording of an elderly or disabled person's declaration of homestead protection, be eligible for protection of such ownership interest to the extent of the declared homestead exemption as set forth in clauses (3) and (4) of the definition of "declared homestead exemption" in section 1 regardless of whether such declaration is recorded individually or jointly with another. (b) Except as provided in the following paragraph, each elderly or disabled person's estate of homestead shall terminate upon: (i) the sale or transfer of that person's ownership interest in the home, except where the elderly or	

State	Description of Property and Amount	Applicability of Federal Exemptions
	disabled person is also the transferee of all or a portion of the transferred interest; (ii) the recorded release of that person's homestead estate; (iii) the subsequent declaration of an estate of homestead on other property; (iv) the abandonment of the home as the principal residence by the person; (v) the death of the person; or (vi) with respect to a home owned in trust, the execution of a deed or recorded release by the trustees. In the event that an owner records a declaration under this section and then conveys to or is survived by a spouse who does not have the benefit of an estate of homestead created under this section or section 3 and the spouse occupies or intends to occupy the home as the principal residence, then the spouse shall be deemed, as of the time such spouse acquired title, to have the benefit of the declaration previously recorded to the same extent as if such declaration had been recorded under section 3, until the spouse becomes eligible for and records a declaration of homestead pursuant to this section. (c) No declaration of homestead created under this section shall terminate the existing homestead rights of a non-titled spouse or any minor children. (d) Nothing in this section shall prohibit an elderly or disabled person from declaring or continuing a homestead pursuant to section 3, but no person shall concurrently hold rights under both this section and section 3.	

Table 1. (Continued)

State	Description of Property and Amount	Applicability of Federal Exemptions
	Mass. Gen. Laws ch. 188, § 3 (2011). Estate of Homestead – Declaration of Homestead [Effective March 16, 2011] (a) An estate of homestead to the extent of the declared homestead exemption in a home may be acquired by 1 or more owners who occupy or intend to occupy the home as a principal residence. The estate of homestead shall be created by a written declaration executed and recorded in accordance with section 5. A homestead declaration shall benefit each owner making the declaration and that owner's family members who occupy or intend to occupy the home as their principal residence. The homestead rights of non-titled family members shall consist of the right to use, occupy and enjoy the home as their principal residence. **Mass. Gen. Laws ch. 188, § 4 (2011). Estate of Homestead – Automatic Homestead Exemption for Principal Residence [Effective March 16, 2011]** In the absence of a valid declaration o f homestead recorded under this chapter, an estate of homestead to the extent of the automatic homestead exemption shall exist in a home for the benefit of the owner and the owner's family members who occupy or intend to occupy the home as a principal residence. The homestead rights of non-titled family members shall consist of the right to use, occupy	

State	Description of Property and Amount	Applicability of Federal Exemptions
	and enjoy the home as a principal residence. The estate shall be held subject to this chapter, except for section 2, subsection (a) of section 3 and section 5. In the event that spouses occupy or intend to occupy separate homes, then both estates of homestead together shall not exceed the automatic homestead exemption. The recording of a declaration of homestead under this chapter shall supersede the automatic homestead exemption provided by this section, but shall not terminate the automatic homestead exemption applicable to the period between the creation of the automatic homestead and the later recording of a declaration of homestead. If a superseding declaration of homestead on the same home is later invalidated or terminated, the estate of homestead provided in this section shall be reinstated as of the date of its original creation. A homestead under this section may be subordinated to a subsequent new loan or line of credit; provided, however, that that new loan or line of credit: (a) is not secured by a recorded document; (b) does not exceed $20,000; (c) is exempt from the provisions of chapter 140D; (d) is evidenced by a written agreement executed by all record owners and their non-titled spouses for the purpose of subordinating the homestead as provided herein; and (e) contains a statement in substantially the following form, in boldface type and of a minimum size of 12-point font, "I understand that homestead property is in many cases	

Table 1. (Continued)

State	Description of Property and Amount	Applicability of Federal Exemptions
	protected from the claims of creditors and exempt from judicial sale; and that by signing this contract, I voluntarily give up my right to this protection for this property with respect to claims up to the principal amount of the loan or line of credit provided under this contract." The subordination allowed in this paragraph shall not apply to credit card agreements or to any loan made in anticipation of a paycheck, tax refund or insurance settlement. **Mass. Gen. Laws ch. 188, § 5 (2011). Estate of Homestead – Formalities [Effective March 16, 2011]** (a) A declaration of homestead shall be in writing, signed and acknowledged under penalty of perjury by each owner to be benefited by the homestead, except as provided in clause (4), shall be recorded and shall comply with the following: (1) each owner to be benefited by the homestead, and the owner's non-titled spouse, if any, shall be identified; (2) the declaration shall state that each person named therein occupies or intends to occupy the home as their principal residence; (3) if the home is co-owned by a married couple, whether in their names only or as co-tenants with others, and the home is the principal residence or is intended to be the principal residence of both spouses, a declaration under section 3	

State	Description of Property and Amount	Applicability of Federal Exemptions
	shall be executed by both spouses; and (4) if the home is owned in trust, only the trustee shall execute the declaration. (b) A declaration of homestead under section 2 shall, in addition to the requirements of subsection (a), include the following: (1) a statement that the owner to be benefited is an elderly person or a disabled person; and (2) with respect to a declaration of homestead benefiting a disabled person: (i) an original or certified copy of a disability award letter issued to the person by the United States Social Security Administration; or (ii) a letter signed by a physician registered with the board of registration in medicine certifying that the person meets the disability requirements stated in 42 U.S.C. 1382c(a)(3)(A) and 42 U.S.C. 1382 c(a)(3)(C) as in effect at the time of recording; provided, however, that the award letter or physician's letter shall be recorded with the declaration. (c) A declaration of homestead shall not be created within a deed or other instrument vesting title in the owner. (d) The statement of principal residence required in clause (2) of subsection (a) shall be binding upon an identified owner, including an owner who is a beneficiary of a trust, but may be overcome by an interested third party upon presentation of clear and convincing evidence to the contrary. In the event that spouses occupy or intend to	

Table 1. (Continued)

State	Description of Property and Amount	Applicability of Federal Exemptions
	occupy separate homes and valid declarations are recorded with respect to each, then both estates of homestead together shall not exceed the declared homestead exemption. The estate of homestead of an individual who records a declaration of homestead under section 3 and who subsequently marries shall automatically be deemed to benefit that individual's spouse. Any subsequent recording of a declaration of homestead benefiting: (i) a family member identified on a prior declaration on the same home; or (ii) the spouse of that person, without an intervening release, shall relate back to the filing date of the earliest recorded declaration, but the provisions of this chapter pursuant to which the later recorded declaration was made shall control the rights of a person identified in the later declaration. **Mass. Gen. Laws ch. 235, § 34 (2011). Property Exempt From Execution [Effective through March 31, 2011]** Fourteenth, Estates of homestead as defined in chapter one hundred and eighty-eight or, in lieu thereof, the amount of money each rental period, not exceeding two hundred dollars per month, necessary to pay the rent for the dwelling unit occupied by him and his family. **Mass. Gen. Laws ch. 235, § 34 (2011). Property Exempt From Execution [Effective April 1, 2011]**	

State	Description of Property and Amount	Applicability of Federal Exemptions
	Fourteenth, Estates of homestead as defined in chapter 188 or, in lieu thereof, the amount of money each rental period, not exceeding $2,500 per month, necessary to pay the rent for the dwelling unit occupied by the debtor and the debtor's family. **An Act Relative to the Estate of Homestead, Mass. Acts, Chap. 395 (Dec. 16, 2010).** SECTION 3. All existing estates of homestead in effect on the effective date of this act shall continue in full force and effect notwithstanding the repeal of any law under which they were created and shall be governed by this act, notwithstanding their failure to comply with the execution requirements of section 5 of chapter 188 of the General Laws, as appearing in section 1 of this act.	
Michigan	Homestead: $3,500 **Mich. Comp. Laws § 600.6023 (2011). Property exempt from levy and sale under execution; lien excluded from exemption; homestead exemption; rents and profits** (1) The following property of the debtor and the debtor's dependents shall be exempt from levy and sale under any execution: (h) A homestead of not exceeding 40 acres of land and the dwelling house and appurtenances on that homestead, and not included in any recorded plat, city, or village, or, instead, and at the option of the owner, a quantity of land not exceeding in amount 1 lot, being within a recorded	No statutory prohibition. Use of federal exemptions permitted.

Table 1. (Continued)

State	Description of Property and Amount	Applicability of Federal Exemptions
	town plat, city, or village, and the dwelling house and appurtenances on that land, owned and occupied by any resident of this state, not exceeding in value $3,500.00. This exemption extends to any person owning and occupying any house on land not his or her own and which the person claims as a homestead. However, this exemption does not apply to any mortgage on the homestead, lawfully obtained, except that the mortgage is not valid without the signature of a married judgment debtor's spouse unless either of the following occurs: (i) The mortgage is given to secure the payment of the purchase money or a portion of the purchase money. (ii) The mortgage is recorded in the office of the register of deeds of the county in which the property is located, for a period of 25 years, and no notice of a claim of invalidity is filed in that office during the 25 years following the recording of the mortgage. (j) The homestead of a family, after the death of the owner of the homestead, from the payment of his or her debts in all cases during the minority of his or her children. **Mich. Comp. Laws § 559.214 (2011). Homestead exemption** The laws of this state relating to the exemption of homestead property from levy and execution shall be applicable to condominium units occupied as homesteads.	

State	Description of Property and Amount	Applicability of Federal Exemptions
Minnesota	Homestead: July 1, 2008 – June 30, 2010: $330,000 unless primarily agricultural; $825,000 if primarily agricultural July 1, 2010 – June 30, 2012: $360,000 unless primarily agricultural; $900,000 if primarily agricultural **Minn. Stat. § 510.02 (2010). Area and value; how limited** Subdivision 1. Exemption. The homestead may include any quantity of land not exceeding 160 acres. The exemption per homestead, whether the exemption is claimed by one or more debtors, may not exceed $300,000 or, if the homestead is used primarily for agricultural purposes, $750,000, exclusive of the limitations set forth in section 510.05. Subd. 2. Adjustment of dollar amounts. The dollar amounts in subdivision 1 must change periodically in the manner provided for under section 550.37, subdivision 4a. The commissioner of commerce shall include the changes in the dollar amounts as part of the announcement and publication made under those provisions. **32 Minn. R. 2226 (2008).** The amount of homestead exemption in *Minnesota Statutes*, Section 510.02 will increase 10% effective July 1,	Use of federal exemptions generally allowed; however, limits may apply to married individuals. **Minn. Stat. § 550.371 (2010). Exemptions in joint bankruptcy** Subdivision 1. Applicable law. Except as provided in this section, the exemptions set forth in subsection (d) of section 522 of the Bankruptcy Act, United States Code, title 11, section 522(d), shall be available to residents of this state. Subd. 2. Joint petition. When a husband and wife are joined in a petition for bankruptcy, they may jointly elect to utilize either the applicable exemption provisions pursuant to Minnesota law or pursuant to subsection (d) of section 522 of the Bankruptcy Act, United States Code, title 11, section 522(d), but not both. Subd. 3. Individual petition. When a petition for bankruptcy is filed individually, and not jointly, for a husband or a wife, (a) one spouse shall not claim any exemption pursuant to Minnesota law for a period of three years from the date of filing if the other spouse has claimed any

Table 1. (Continued)

State	Description of Property and Amount	Applicability of Federal Exemptions
	2008. This statute require [sic] that the dollar amounts be adjusted in even numbered years based on a percentage change in the Implicit Price Deflator for the Gross National Product. Homestead $330,000 Homestead for agricultural purposes $825,000 The next published adjustment is scheduled on or before April 30, 2010, for July 1, 2010 based on the December 2009 index. **24 Minn. R. 1460 (2010).** [T]he homestead exemption in *Minnesota Statutes*, Section 510.02 will increase 10% effective July 1, 2010. [This statute] require[s] that the dollar amounts be adjusted in even numbered years based on a percentage change in the Implicit Price Deflator for the Gross National Product. Homestead $360,000 Homestead for agricultural purposes $900,000 The next published adjustment is scheduled on or before April 30, 2012, for July 1, 2012 based on the December 2011 index.	exemption under subsection (d) of section 522 of the Bankruptcy Act, United States Code, title 11, section 522(d); and (b) one spouse shall not claim any exemption pursuant to subsection (d) of section 522 of the Bankruptcy Act, United States Code, title 11, section 522(d), for a period of three years from the date of filing if the other spouse has claimed any exemption pursuant to Minnesota law. Subd. 4. Marital status determined. For the purposes of this section, persons shall be considered to be husband and wife if they are married to each other at the time of the filing of the first individual or joint petition for bankruptcy by either of them unless a decree of separation or temporary order of separation of the parties is issued prior to the time the petition is filed.

State	Description of Property and Amount	Applicability of Federal Exemptions
Mississippi	Homestead: $75,000 if real property; $30,000 if personal property **Miss. Code Ann. § 85-3-1 (2011). Property exempt from seizure under execution or attachment** There shall be exempt from seizure under execution or attachment: (d) One (1) mobile home, trailer, manufactured housing, or similar type dwelling owned and occupied as the primary residence by the debtor, not exceeding a value of Thirty Thousand Dollars ($30,000.00); in determining this value, existing encumbrances on the dwelling, including taxes and all other liens, shall first be deducted from the actual value of the dwelling. A debtor is not entitled to the exemption of a mobile home as personal property who claims a homestead exemption under Section 85-3-21, and the exemption shall not apply to collection of delinquent taxes under Sections 27-41-101 through 27-41-109. **Miss. Code Ann. § 85-3-21 (2011). Homestead exemption; land and buildings** Every citizen of this state, male or female, being a householder shall be entitled to hold exempt from seizure or sale, under execution or attachment, the land and buildings owned and occupied as a residence by him, or her, but the quantity of land shall not exceed one hundred sixty (160) acres, nor the value thereof, inclusive of improvements, save as hereinafter provided, the sum of	Federal exemptions *not* permitted. **Miss. Code Ann. § 85-3-2 (2011). Certain federal exemptions prohibited** In accordance with the provisions of Section 522(b) of the Bankruptcy Reform Act of 1978, as amended (11 U.S.C.S. 522(b)), residents of the State of Mississippi shall not be entitled to the federal exemptions provided in Section 522(d) of the Bankruptcy Reform Act of 1978, as amended (11 U.S.C.S. 522(d)). Nothing in this section shall affect the exemptions given to individuals of Mississippi by the Constitution and statutes of the State of Mississippi.

Table 1. (Continued)

State	Description of Property and Amount	Applicability of Federal Exemptions
	Seventy-five Thousand Dollars ($75,000.00); provided, however, that in determining this value, existing encumbrances on such land and buildings, including taxes and all other liens, shall first be deducted from the actual value of such land and buildings. But husband or wife, widower or widow, over sixty (60) years of age, who has been an exemptionist under this section, shall not be deprived of such exemption because of not residing therein.	
Missouri	Homestead: $15,000; $5,000 if mobile home not on or attached to land owned by debtor. **Mo. Rev. Stat. § 513.430 (2011). Property exempt from attachment—benefits from certain employee plans, exception—bankruptcy proceeding, fraudulent transfers, exception—construction of section** 1. The following property shall be exempt from attachment and execution to the extent of any person's interest therein: (3) Any other property of any kind, not to exceed in value six hundred dollars in the aggregate; … (6) Any mobile home used as the principal residence but not on or attached to real property in which the debtor has a fee interest, not to exceed five thousand dollars in value; **Mo. Rev. Stat. § 513.475 (2011). Homestead defined—exempt from execution—spouses debarred from selling, when**	Federal exemptions *not* permitted. **Mo. Rev. Stat. § 513.427 (2011). Bankruptcy, exemptions allowed** Every person by or against whom an order is sought for relief under Title 11, United States Code, shall be permitted to exempt from property of the estate any property that is exempt from attachment and execution under the law of the state of Missouri or under federal law, other than Title 11, United States Code, Section 522(d), and no such person is authorized to claim as exempt the property that is specified under Title 11, United States Code, Section 522(d).

State	Description of Property and Amount	Applicability of Federal Exemptions
	1. The homestead of every person, consisting of a dwelling house and appurtenances, and the land used in connection therewith, not exceeding the value of fifteen thousand dollars, which is or shall be used by such person as a homestead, shall, together with the rents, issues and products thereof, be exempt from attachment and execution. The exemption allowed under this section shall not be allowed for more than one owner of any homestead if one owner claims the entire amount allowed under this subsection; but, if more than one owner of any homestead claims an exemption under this section, the exemption allowed to each of such owners shall not exceed, in the aggregate, the total exemption allowed under this subsection as to any one homestead.	
Montana	Homestead: $250,000, but proportional to undivided interest in real property **Mont. Code Ann. § 70-32-101 (2010). Of what homestead consists** The homestead consists of the dwelling house or mobile home, and all appurtenances, in which the claimant resides and the land, if any, on which the same is situated, selected as provided in this chapter. **Mont. Code Ann. § 70-32-104 (2010). Limitation on value** (1) A homestead may not exceed $250,000 in value. In a proceeding instituted to determine the value of the	Federal exemptions *not* permitted. **Mont. Code Ann. § 31-2-106 (2010). Exempt property— bankruptcy proceeding** An individual may not exempt from the property of the estate in any bankruptcy proceeding the property specified in 11 U.S.C. 522(d). An individual may exempt from the property of the estate in any bankruptcy proceeding: (1) that property exempt from execution of judgment as provided in 19-2-1004, 19-18-

Table 1. (Continued)

State	Description of Property and Amount	Applicability of Federal Exemptions
	homestead, the assessed value of the land with included appurtenances, if any, and of the dwelling house as it appears on the last-completed assessment roll preceding the institution of the proceeding is prima facie evidence of the value of the property claimed as a homestead. (2) If a claimant who is an owner of an undivided interest in real property claims a homestead exemption, the claimant is limited to an exemption amount proportional to the claimant's undivided interest.	612, 19-19-504, 19-20-706, 19-21-212, Title 25, chapter 13, part 6, 33-7-522, 33-15-512 through 33-15-514, 39-51-3105, 39-71-743, 39-73-110, 53-2-607, 53-9-129, Title 70, chapter 32, and 80-2-245.
Nebraska	Homestead: $60,000 **Neb. Rev. Stat. § 40-101 (2011). Homestead, defined; exempted** A homestead not exceeding sixty thousand dollars in value shall consist of the dwelling house in which the claimant resides, its appurtenances, and the land on which the same is situated, not exceeding one hundred and sixty acres of land, to be selected by the owner, and not in any incorporated city or village, or, at the option of the claimant, a quantity of contiguous land not exceeding two lots within any incorporated city or village, and shall be exempt from judgment liens and from execution or forced sale, except as provided in sections 40-101 to 40-116.	Federal exemptions *not* permitted. **Neb. Rev. Stat. § 25-15,105 (2011). Federal exemptions; rejected** The federal exemptions provided in 11 U.S.C. 522, subsection (d), are hereby rejected by the State of Nebraska. The State of Nebraska elects to retain the personal exemptions provided under Nebraska statutes and the Nebraska Constitution and to have such exemptions apply to any bankruptcy petition filed in Nebraska after April 17, 1980.

State	Description of Property and Amount	Applicability of Federal Exemptions
Nevada	Homestead: $550,000; however, unlimited if allodial title has been established **Nev. Const. Art. 4, § 30 (2011). Homesteads: Exemption from forced sale; joint consent required for alienation; recording of declaration** A homestead as provided by law, shall be exempt from forced sale under any process of law, and shall not be alienated without the joint consent of husband and wife when that relation exists; but no property shall be exempt from sale for taxes or for the payment of obligations contracted for the purchase of said premises, or for the erection of improvements thereon; Provided, the provisions of this Section shall not apply to any process of law obtained by virtue of a lien given by the consent of both husband and wife, and laws shall be enacted providing for the recording of such homestead within the County in which the same shall be situated. **Nev. Rev. Stat. Ann. § 21.090 (2011). Property exempt from execution** 1. The following property is exempt from execution, except as otherwise specifically provided in this section or required by federal law: (l) The homestead as provided for by law, including a homestead for which allodial title has been established and not relinquished and for which a waiver executed pursuant to NRS 115.010 is not applicable.	Federal exemptions *not* permitted. **Nev. Rev. Stat. Ann. § 21.090 (2011). Property exempt from execution** 3. Any exemptions specified in subsection (d) of section 522 of the Bankruptcy Act of 1978, 11 U.S.C. § 522(d), do not apply to property owned by a resident of this State unless conferred also by subsection 1, as limited by subsection 2.

Table 1. (Continued)

State	Description of Property and Amount	Applicability of Federal Exemptions
	(m) The dwelling of the judgment debtor occupied as a home for himself and family, where the amount of equity held by the judgment debtor in the home does not exceed $550,000 in value and the dwelling is situated upon lands not owned by him. (z) Any personal property not otherwise exempt from execution pursuant to this subsection belonging to the judgment debtor, including, without limitation, the judgment debtor's equity in any property, money, stocks, bonds or other funds on deposit with a financial institution, not to exceed $1,000 in total value, to be selected by the judgment debtor. **Nev. Rev. Stat. Ann. §115.005 (2011). Definitions** As used in this chapter, unless the context otherwise requires: 2. "Homestead" means the property consisting of: (a) A quantity of land, together with the dwelling house thereon and its appurtenances; (b) A mobile home whether or not the underlying land is owned by the claimant; or (c) A unit, whether real or personal property, existing pursuant to chapter 116 or 117 of NRS, with any appurtenant limited common elements and its interest in the common elements of the common-interest community, to be selected by the husband and wife, or either of them, or	

State	Description of Property and Amount	Applicability of Federal Exemptions
	a single person claiming the homestead. **Nev. Rev. Stat. Ann. § 115.010 (2011). Exemption from sale on execution and from process of court; amount of exemption; exceptions; extension of exemption** 1. The homestead is not subject to forced sale on execution or any final process from any court, except as otherwise provided by subsections 2, 3 and 5, and NRS 115.090 and except as otherwise required by federal law. 2. The exemption provided in subsection 1 extends only to that amount of equity in the property held by the claimant which does not exceed $550,000 in value, unless allodial title has been established and not relinquished, in which case the exemption provided in subsection 1 extends to all equity in the dwelling, its appurtenances and the land on which it is located.	
New Hampshire	Homestead: $100,000 **N.H. Rev. Stat. Ann. § 480:1 (2011). Amount** Every person is entitled to $100,000 worth of his or her homestead, or of his or her interest therein, as a homestead. The homestead right created by this chapter shall exist in manufactured housing, as defined by RSA 674:31, which is owned and occupied as a dwelling by the same person but shall not exist in the land upon which the manufactured housing is situated if that land is not also owned by the owner of the manufactured housing.	No statutory prohibition. Use of federal exemptions permitted.

Table 1. (Continued)

State	Description of Property and Amount	Applicability of Federal Exemptions
New Jersey	No specific homestead exemption Wildcard: $1,000, which appears not to extend to real property **N.J. Rev. Stat. § 2A:17-19 (2011). Amount; exceptions** Goods and chattels, shares of stock or interests in any corporation and personal property of every kind, not exceeding in value, exclusive of wearing apparel, $1,000.00, and all wearing apparel, the property of a debtor shall be reserved, both before and after his death, for his use or that of his family or his estate, and shall not be liable to be seized or taken by virtue of any execution or civil process whatever, issued out of any court of this State.	No statutory prohibition. Use of federal exemptions permitted.
New Mexico	Homestead: $60,000 **N.M. Stat. Ann. § 42-10-9 (2011). Homestead exemption** Each person shall have exempt a homestead in a dwelling house and land occupied by the person or in a dwelling house occupied by the person although the dwelling is on land owned by another, provided that the dwelling is owned, leased or being purchased by the person claiming the exemption. Such a person has a homestead of sixty thousand dollars ($60,000) exempt from attachment, execution or foreclosure by a judgment creditor and from any proceeding of receivers or trustees in insolvency proceedings and from executors or administrators in	No statutory prohibition. Use of federal exemptions permitted.

State	Description of Property and Amount	Applicability of Federal Exemptions
	probate. If the homestead is owned jointly by two persons, each joint owner is entitled to an exemption of sixty thousand dollars ($60,000).	
New York	Homestead: $50,000 prior to January 21, 2011. Effective January 21, 2011: $75,000 – $150,000 **N.Y. C.P.L.R. Law § 5206 (2011). Real property exempt from application to the satisfaction of money judgments [Effective before January 21, 2011]** (a) Exemption of homestead. Property of one of the following types, not exceeding fifty thousand dollars in value above liens and encumbrances, owned and occupied as a principal residence, is exempt from application to the satisfaction of a money judgment, unless the judgment was recovered wholly for the purchase price thereof: 1. a lot of land with a dwelling thereon, 2. shares of stock in a cooperative apartment corporation, 3. units of a condominium apartment, or 4. a mobile home. **N.Y. C.P.L.R. Law § 5206 (2011). Real property exempt from application to the satisfaction of money judgments [Effective January 21, 2011]** (a) Exemption of homestead. Property of one of the following types, not exceeding one hundred fifty thousand dollars for the counties of Kings, Queens, New York, Bronx, Richmond, Nassau, Suffolk, Rockland, Westchester and Putnam; one hundred twenty-five thousand dollars for	Federal exemptions *not* permitted. **N.Y. Debt. & Cred. Law § 284 (2011). Exclusivity of exemptions** In accordance with the provisions of section five hundred twenty-two (b) of title eleven of the United States Code, debtors domiciled in this state are not authorized to exempt from the estate property that is specified under subsection (d) of such section.

Table 1. (Continued)

State	Description of Property and Amount	Applicability of Federal Exemptions
	the counties of Dutchess, Albany, Columbia, Orange, Saratoga and Ulster; and seventy-five thousand dollars for the remaining counties of the state in value above liens and encumbrances, owned and occupied as a principal residence, is exempt from application to the satisfaction of a money judgment, unless the judgment was recovered wholly for the purchase price thereof: 1. a lot of land with a dwelling thereon, 2. shares of stock in a cooperative apartment corporation, 3. units of a condominium apartment, or 4. a mobile home. But no exempt homestead shall be exempt from taxation or from sale for non-payment of taxes or assessments.	
North Carolina	Homestead: $35,000 generally; $65,000 for certain individuals age 65 or older. See statute. **N.C. Gen. Stat. § 1C-1601 (2011). What property exempt; waiver; exceptions** (a) Exempt property.—Each individual, resident of this State, who is a debtor is entitled to retain free of the enforcement of the claims of creditors: (1) The debtor's aggregate interest, not to exceed thirty-five thousand dollars ($35,000) in value, in real property or personal property that the debtor or a dependent of the debtor uses as a residence, in a cooperative that owns property that the debtor or a dependent of the debtor uses as	Federal exemptions *not* permitted. **N.C. Gen. Stat. § 1C-1601 (2011). What property exempt; waiver; exceptions** (f) Federal Bankruptcy Code.— The exemptions provided in The Bankruptcy Code, 11 U.S.C. § 522(d), are not applicable to residents of this State. The exemptions provided by this Article and by other statutory or common law of this State shall apply for purposes of The Bankruptcy Code, 11 U.S.C. § 522(b).

State	Description of Property and Amount	Applicability of Federal Exemptions
	a residence, or in a burial plot for the debtor or a dependent of the debtor; however, an unmarried debtor who is 65 years of age or older is entitled to retain an aggregate interest in the property not to exceed sixty thousand dollars ($60,000) in value so long as the property was previously owned by the debtor as a tenant by the entireties or as a joint tenant with rights of survivorship and the former co-owner of the property is deceased.	
North Dakota	Homestead: $100,000 **N.D. Cent. Code § 28-22-02 (2011). Absolute exemption** The property mentioned in this section is absolutely exempt from all process, levy, or sale: 7. The homestead as created, defined, and limited by law. 10. In lieu of the homestead, and subject to the same value limitations that exist with respect to the homestead exemption, any housetrailer or mobile home occupied as a residence by the debtor or the debtor's family, except that it is not exempt from process, levy, or sale for taxes levied on it pursuant to chapter 57-55. This section does not preclude the debtor from claiming a mobile home as a dwelling house as part of the homestead. **N.D. Cent. Code § 47-18-01 (2011). Homestead exemption—Area and value** The homestead of any individual, whether married or unmarried, residing in this state consists of the land upon which the claimant resides, and the dwelling house on	Federal exemptions *not* permitted. **N.D. Cent. Code § 28-22-17 (2011). Nonavailability of federal bankruptcy exemptions.** In accordance with the provisions of section 522(b) of the Bankruptcy Reform Act of 1978 P.L. 95-598; 92 Stat. 2586; 11 U.S.C. 522(b), residents of this state are not entitled to the federal exemptions provided in section 522(d) of the Bankruptcy Reform Act of 1978. The residents of this state are limited to claiming those exemptions allowable by North Dakota law.

Table 1. (Continued)

State	Description of Property and Amount	Applicability of Federal Exemptions
	that land in which the homestead claimant resides, with all its appurtenances, and all other improvements on the land, the total not to exceed one hundred thousand dollars in value, over and above liens or encumbrances or both. The homestead shall be exempt from judgment lien and from execution or forced sale, except as otherwise provided in this chapter. The homestead may not embrace different lots or tracts of land unless the lots or tracts of land are contiguous. For purposes of this section, "contiguous" means two or more tracts of real property which share a common point or which would share a common point but for an intervening road or right of way.	
Ohio	Homestead: $20,200 before April 1, 2010; $21,625 April 1, 2010 through March 31, 2013[d] Wildcard: $1,075 before April 1, 2010; $1,150 April 1, 2010 through March 31, 2013[d] **Ohio Rev. Code Ann. § 2329.66 (2011).**[e] **Exempted interests and rights** (A) Every person who is domiciled in this state may hold property exempt from execution, garnishment, attachment, or sale to satisfy a judgment or order, as follows: (1)(a) In the case of a judgment or order regarding money owed for health care services rendered or health care supplies provided to the person or a dependent of the person, one parcel or item of real or personal property	Federal exemptions *not* permitted. **Ohio Rev. Code Ann. § 2329.662(2011).** **Federal exemption not authorized** Pursuant to the "Bankruptcy Reform Act of 1978," 92 Stat. 2549, 11 U.S.C. 522(b)(1), this state specifically does not authorize debtors who are domiciled in this state to exempt the property specified in the "Bankruptcy Reform Act of 1978," 92 Stat. 2549, 11 U.S.C. 522(d).

State	Description of Property and Amount	Applicability of Federal Exemptions
	that the person or a dependent of the person uses as a residence. Division (A)(1)(a) of this section does not preclude, affect, or invalidate the creation under this chapter of a judgment lien upon the exempted property but only delays the enforcement of the lien until the property is sold or otherwise transferred by the owner or in accordance with other applicable laws to a person or entity other than the surviving spouse or surviving minor children of the judgment debtor. Every person who is domiciled in this state may hold exempt from a judgment lien created pursuant to division (A)(1)(a) of this section the person's interest, not to exceed twenty thousand two hundred dollars, in the exempted property. (b) In the case of all other judgments and orders, the person's interest, not to exceed twenty thousand two hundred dollars, in one parcel or item of real or personal property that the person or a dependent of the person uses as a residence. (18) The person's aggregate interest in any property, not to exceed one thousand seventy-five dollars, except that division (A)(18) of this section applies only in bankruptcy proceedings. (B) On April 1, 2010,[d] and on the first day of April in each third calendar year after 2010, each dollar amount set forth in this section shall be adjusted, when determining the amount that is exempt from execution, garnishment,	

Table 1. (Continued)

State	Description of Property and Amount	Applicability of Federal Exemptions
	attachment, or sale pursuant to this section, to reflect the change in the consumer price index for all urban consumers, as published by the United States dep-artment of labor, or, if that index is no longer published, a generally available comparable index, for the three-year period ending on the thirty-first day of December of the receding year. Any adjustments required by this division shall be rounded to the nearest twenty-five dollars.	
Oklahoma	Homestead: Unlimited dollar amount **Okla. Stat. Ann. tit. 31, § 1 (2011). Property exempt from attachment, execution or other forced sale—Bankruptcy proceedings** A. Except as otherwise provided in this title and notwithstanding subsection B of this section, the following property shall be reserved to every personresiding in the state, exempt from attachment or execution and every other species of forced sale for the payment of debts, except as herein provided: 1. The home of such person, provided that such home is the principal residence of such person; 2. A manufactured home, provided that such manufactured home is the principal residence of such person. **Okla. Stat. Ann. tit. 31, § 2 (2011). Homestead—Area and value—Indian allottees—Temporary renting**	Federal exemptions *not* permitted. **Okla. Stat. Ann. tit. 31, § 1 (2011). Property exempt from attachment, execution or other forced sale—Bankruptcy proceedings** B. No natural person residing in this state may exempt from the property of the estate in any bankruptcy proceeding the property specified in subsection (d) of Section 522 of the Bankruptcy Reform Act of 1978, P.L. 95-598, 11 U.S.C.A. 101 et seq., except as may otherwise be expressly permitted under this title or other statutes of this state.

State	Description of Property and Amount	Applicability of Federal Exemptions
	A. The homestead of any person in this state, not within any city or town, shall consist of not more than one hundred sixty (160) acres of land, which may be in one or more parcels, to be selected by the owner. B. Effective November 1, 1997, the homestead of any person in this state, not within any city or town, annexed by a city or town on or after November 1, 1997, owned and occupied and used for both residential and commercial agricultural purposes shall consist of not more than one hundred sixty (160) acres of land, which may be in one or more parcels, to be selected by the owner. C. The homestead of any person within any city or town, owned and occupied as a residence only, or used for both residential and business purposes, shall consist of not exceeding one (1) acre of land, to be selected by the owner. For purposes of this subsection, at least seventy-five percent (75%) of the total square foot area of the improvements for which a homestead exemption is claimed must be used as the principal residence in order to qualify for the exemption. If more than twenty-five percent (25%) of the total square foot area of the improvements for which a homestead exemption is claimed is used for business purposes, the homestead exemption amount shall not exceed Five Thousand Dollars ($ 5,000.00).	
Oregon	Homestead: $40,000-$50,000 depending on facts and circumstances. See statute.	Federal exemptions *not* permitted. **Or. Rev. Stat. § 18.300 (2010). Resident**

Table 1. (Continued)

State	Description of Property and Amount	Applicability of Federal Exemptions
	Or. Rev. Stat. § 18.395 (2010). Homestead exemption (1) A homestead shall be exempt from sale on execution, from the lien of every judgment and from liability in any form for the debts of the owner to the amount in value of $40,000, except as otherwise provided by law. The exemption shall be effective without the necessity of a claim thereof by the judgment debtor. When two or more members of a household are debtors whose interests in the homestead are subject to sale on execution, the lien of a judgment or liability in any form, their combined exemptions under this section shall not exceed $50,000. The homestead must be the actual abode of and occupied by the owner, or the owner's spouse, parent or child, but the exemption shall not be impaired by: (a) Temporary removal or temporary absence with the intention to reoccupy the same as a homestead; (b) Removal or absence from the property; or (c) The sale of the property. **Or. Rev. Stat. § 18.402 (2010). Limitations on homestead exemption** The homestead mentioned in ORS 18.395 shall consist, when not located in any town or city laid off into blocks and lots, of any quantity of land not exceeding 160 acres, and when located in any such town or city, of any quantity of land not exceeding one block. However, a	**not entitled to federal bankruptcy exemptions** In accordance with Section 522 (b) of the Bankruptcy Code of 1978 (11 U.S.C. 522 (b)), residents of this state shall not be entitled to the federal exemptions provided in Section 522 (d) of the Bankruptcy Code of 1978 (11 U.S.C. 522 (d)). Nothing in this section shall affect the exemptions given to residents of this state by the Constitution of the State of Oregon and the Oregon Revised Statutes.

State	Description of Property and Amount	Applicability of Federal Exemptions
	homestead under this section shall not exceed in value the sum of $40,000 or $50,000, whichever amount is applicable under ORS 18.395 (1).	
Pennsylvania	No specific homestead provision. Wildcard: $300 **42 Pa. Cons. Stat. § 8123 (2011). General monetary exemption** (a) GENERAL RULE.—In addition to any other property specifically exempted by this subchapter, property of the judgment debtor (including bank notes, money, securities, real property, judgments or other indebtedness due the judgment debtor) to the value of $300 shall be exempt from attachment or execution on a judgment. Within such time as may be prescribed by general rules the judgment debtor may claim the exemption in kind and may designate the specific items of property to which the exemption provided by this section shall be applicable unless the designated property is not capable of appropriate division, or the judgment debtor may claim the exemption in cash out of the proceeds of the sale.	No statutory prohibition. Use of federal exemptions permitted.
Rhode Island	Homestead: $300,000 **R.I. Gen. Laws § 9-26-4.1 (2011). Homestead estate exemption** (a) In addition to the property exempt from attachment as set forth in § 9-26-4, an estate of homestead to the extent of three hundred thousand dollars ($300,000) in the land and	No statutory prohibition. Use of federal exemptions permitted.

Table 1. (Continued)

State	Description of Property and Amount	Applicability of Federal Exemptions
	buildings may be acquired pursuant to this section by an owner or owners of a home or one or all who rightfully possess the premise by lease or otherwise, and who occupy or intend to occupy the home as a principal residence. The estate of homestead provided pursuant to this section shall be automatic by operation of law, and without any requirement or necessity for the filing of a declaration, a statement in a deed, or any other documentation. The estate shall be exempt from the laws of attachment, levy on execution and sale for payment of debts or legacies except in the following cases: (1) Sale for taxes, sewer liens, water liens, lighting district assessments and fire district assessments; (2) For a debt contracted prior to the acquisition of the estate of homestead; (3) For a debt contracted for the purchase of the home; (4) Upon an order issued by the family court to enforce its judgment that a spouse pay a certain amount weekly or otherwise for the support of a spouse or minor children; (5) Where a building or buildings are situated on land not owned by the owner of a homestead estate are attached, levied upon or sold for the ground rent of the lot upon which the building or buildings are situated; (6) for a debt due to, or a lien in favor of, the department of human services and/or the state of Rhode	

State	Description of Property and Amount	Applicability of Federal Exemptions
	Island for reimbursement of medical assistance, as provided for in § 40-8-15; (7) For a debt heretofore or hereafter owing to a federally insured deposit taking institution or a person regulated or licensed under title 19. (b) For the purposes of this section, "owner of a home" includes a sole owner, joint tenant, tenant by the entirety or tenant in common, provided, that only one owner may acquire an estate in a homestead in any such home for the benefit of his or her family; and provided further, that an estate of homestead may be acquired on only one principal residence for the benefit of a family. For the purposes of this chapter, the word "family" includes either a parent and child or children, a husband and wife and their children, if any, or a sole owner. The provisions of this section shall not apply to any debt owing to a financial institution, or private mortgages, or a mechanics' lien on the property comprising the estate as provided for under chapter 28 of title 34. Notwithstanding any other provisions of law, it shall not be necessary to record a declaration of homestead in order to take advantage of the homestead estate exemption.	
South Carolina	Homestead: Effective July 7, 2010, $53,375; $106,750 if multiple exemptions, but each is adjusted biannually **S.C. Code Ann. § 15-41-30 (2010). Property exempt from attachment, levy, and sale**	Federal exemptions *not* permitted. **S.C. Code Ann. § 15-41-35 (2010). Exempt property**

Table 1. (Continued)

State	Description of Property and Amount	Applicability of Federal Exemptions
	(A) The following real and personal property of a debtor domiciled in this State is exempt from attachment, levy, and sale under any mesne or final process issued by a court or bankruptcy proceeding: (1) The debtor's aggregate interest, not to exceed fifty thousand dollars in value, in real property or personal property that the debtor or a dependent of the debtor uses as a residence, in a cooperative that owns property that the debtor or a dependent of the debtor uses as a residence, or in a burial plot for the debtor or a dependent of the debtor, except that the aggregate value of multiple homestead exemptions allowable with respect to a single living unit may not exceed one hundred thousand dollars. If there are multiple owners of such a living unit exempt as a homestead, the value of the exemption of each individual owner may not exceed his fractional portion of one hundred thousand dollars. (B) Beginning on July 1, 2008, and each even-numbered year thereafter, each dollar amount in subsection (A), items (1) through (14), immediately before July first, must be adjusted to reflect the change in the Southeastern Consumer Price Index, All Urban Consumers, as published by the Department of Labor, Bureau of Labor Statistics, for the most recent year ending immediately before January first preceding July first, and to round to the nearest twenty-	No individual may exempt from the property of the estate in any bankruptcy proceeding the property specified in 11 U.S.C. Section 522(d) except as may be expressly permitted by this chapter or by other provisions of law of this State.

State	Description of Property and Amount	Applicability of Federal Exemptions
	five dollars, the dollar amount that represents this change. No later than March first of each even-numbered year, the Economic Research Section of the Office of Research and Statistics of the State Budget and Control Board shall publish in the State Register the dollar amounts that will become effective on July first of each even-numbered year. **34-5 S.C. Reg. 5 (March 28, 2010).** **Budget and Control Board Office of Research and Statistics—Notice** Pursuant to the South Carolina Code of Laws, Section 15-41-30 requires the Economic Research Section of the Office of Research and Statistics of the Budget and Control Board to adjust each dollar amount in subsection A, items (1) through (14), by the change in the Southeastern Consumer Price Index, All Urban Consumers, as published by the U.S. Department of Labor Statistics, for the most recent year ending immediately before January first preceding July first. We computed the change in the index as the change in the average value of the index for the period from January 1 2009 through December 31, 2009 compared to the average value of the index for the period from January 1, 2006 through December 31, 2006. This percentage change was 6.8 percent. Each dollar amount that represents this change has been rounded to the nearest twenty-five dollars as required by law. I have enclosed a table for you that represents the changes that should be	

Table 1. (Continued)

<table>
<tr><th>State</th><th>Description of Property and Amount</th><th>Applicability of Federal Exemptions</th></tr>
<tr><td></td><td>made to each dollar amount in Section 15-41-30(A)(1) through (14).
Section 15-41-30. Property Exempt from Attachment, Levy, and Sales
<table><tr><th>Subsection</th><th>Amount Specified as of May 22, 2008</th><th>Adjusted for Inflation</th></tr><tr><td>1</td><td>$50,000</td><td>$53,375</td></tr><tr><td></td><td>$100,000</td><td>$106,750</td></tr></table></td><td></td></tr>
<tr><td>South Dakota</td><td>Homestead: Unlimited dollar amount
S.D. Codified Laws § 43-31-1 (2011). Homestead
The homestead of every family, resident in this state, as hereinafter defined, so long as it continues to possess the character of a homestead is exempt from judicial sale, from judgment lien, and from all mesne or final process from any court, to the extent and as provided by statute. However, a creditor or lien holder of a mobile home classified as a homestead under § 43-31-2 prior to January 1, 1973, may not be cut off and is not subject to a homestead exemption. In addition, a homestead with a value of less than one hundred seventy thousand dollars of a person seventy years of age or older, and the unremarried surviving spouse of such person, is exempt from sale for taxes for so long as it continues to possess</td><td>Federal exemptions not permitted.
S.D. Codified Laws § 43-31-30 (2011).
In accordance with the provision of § 522(b) of the Bankruptcy Code of 1978 (11 U.S.C. § 522(b)), residents of this state are not entitled to the federal exemptions provided in § 522(d) of the Bankruptcy Code of 1978 (11 U.S.C. § 522(d)), exemptions which this state specifically does not authorize. Nothing herein affects the exemptions given to residents of this state by the state Constitution and</td></tr>
</table>

State	Description of Property and Amount	Applicability of Federal Exemptions
	the character of a homestead. **S.D. Codified Laws § 43-31-2 (2011).** The homestead must embrace the house used as a home by the owner thereof, being either, real property or a mobile home as hereinafter defined, and if he or she has two or more houses or mobile homes thus used at different times and places, such owner may select which he or she will retain as a homestead. It must not embrace more than one dwelling house or any other buildings except such as are properly appurtenant to the homestead as such; but a shop, store, or other building situated on real property and really used or occupied by the owner in the prosecution of his own ordinary business may be deemed appurtenant to such homestead. Mobile homes shall include any vehicle without motive power which can provide adequate, comfortable, all season quarters for the purpose of making a residence thereof and which vehicle is larger than two hundred forty square feet, measuring at the base thereof. Such mobile home must be registered in South Dakota at least six months prior to the claim of exemption. **S.D. Codified Laws § 43-31-4 (2011).** If within a town plat the homestead must not exceed one acre in extent, and if not within a town plat, it must not embrace in the aggregate more than one hundred sixty acres. If the homestead is claimed upon any land, the title	the South Dakota statutes. **S.D. Codified Laws § 43-45-13 (2011).** In accordance with the provision of § 522(b) of the Bankruptcy Code of 1978 (11 U.S.C. § 522(b)), residents of this state are not entitled to the federal exemptions provided in § 522(d) of the Bankruptcy Code of 1978 (11 U.S.C. § 522(d)), exemptions which this state specifically does not authorize. Nothing herein affects the exemptions given to residents of this state by the state Constitution and the South Dakota statutes.

Table 1. (Continued)

State	Description of Property and Amount	Applicability of Federal Exemptions
	or right of possession to which was acquired or claimed under the laws of the United States, relating to mineral lands, then the area of the homestead, if within a town plat, shall not exceed one acre, and if without a town plat it must not exceed forty acres, if title thereto has been acquired as a placer claim, but if the title has been acquired under the laws of Congress as a lode mining claim, the area of such homestead shall not exceed five acres. **S.D. Codified Laws § 43-45-3 (2011). Homestead absolutely exempt—Extent of exemption when homestead sold** A homestead: (1) As defined and limited in chapter 43-31, is absolutely exempt; or (2) In the event such homestead is sold under the provisions of chapter 21-19, or is sold by the owner voluntarily, the proceeds of such sale, not exceeding the sum of sixty thousand dollars, is absolutely exempt for a period of one year after the receipt of such proceeds by the owner. Such exemption shall be limited to one hundred seventy thousand dollars for a homestead of a person seventy years of age or older or the unremarried surviving spouse of such person so long as it continues to possess the character of a homestead.	

State	Description of Property and Amount	Applicability of Federal Exemptions
Tennessee	Homestead: $5,000-$25,000 depending on facts and circumstances. See statute. **Tenn. Code Ann. § 26-2-301 (2011). Basic exemption** (a) An individual, whether a head of family or not, shall be entitled to a homestead exemption upon real property which is owned by the individual and used by the individual or the individual's spouse or dependent, as a principal place of residence. The aggregate value of such homestead exemption shall not exceed five thousand dollars ($5,000); provided, individuals who jointly own and use real property as their principal place of residence shall be entitled to homestead exemptions, the aggregate value of which exemptions combined shall not exceed seven thousand five hundred dollars ($7,500), which shall be divided equally among them in the event the homestead exemptions are claimed in the same proceeding; provided, if only one (1) of the joint owners of real property used as their principal place of residence is involved in the proceeding wherein homestead exemption is claimed, then the individual's homestead exemption shall be five thousand dollars ($5,000). The homestead exemption shall not be subject to execution, attachment, or sale under legal proceedings during the life of the individual. Upon the death of an individual who is head of a family, any such exemption shall inure to the benefit of the surviving spouse and their minor children for as long as the spouse or the minor children use such property as a principal place of residence.	Federal exemptions *not* permitted. **Tenn. Code Ann. § 26-2-112 (2011). Exemptions for the purpose of bankruptcy** The personal property exemptions as provided for in this part, and the other exemptions as provided in other sections of the Tennessee Code Annotated for the citizens of Tennessee, are hereby declared adequate and the citizens of Tennessee, pursuant to section 522 (b) (1), P.L. 95-598 known as the Bankruptcy Reform Act of 1978, Title 11 USC, section 522 (b) (1), are not authorized to claim as exempt the property described in the Bankruptcy Reform Act of 1978, 11 USC 522 (d).

Table 1. (Continued)

State	Description of Property and Amount	Applicability of Federal Exemptions
	(e) Notwithstanding the provisions of subsection (a) to the contrary, an unmarried individual who is sixty-two (62) years of age or older shall be entitled to a homestead exemption not exceeding twelve thousand five hundred dollars ($12,500) upon real property that is owned by the individual and used by the individual as a principal place of residence; a married couple, one (1) of whom is sixty-two (62) years of age or older and the other of whom is younger than sixty-two (62) years of age, shall be entitled to a homestead exemption not exceeding twenty thousand dollars ($20,000) upon real property that is owned by one (1) or both of the members of the couple and used by the couple as their principal place of residence; and a married couple, both of whom are sixty-two (62) years of age or older, shall be entitled to a homestead exemption not exceeding twenty-five thousand dollars ($25,000) upon real property that is owned by one (1) or both of the members of the couple and used by the couple as their principal place of residence. (f) Notwithstanding subsection (a) to the contrary, an individual who has one (1) or more minor children in the individual's custody shall be entitled to a homestead exemption not exceeding twenty-five thousand dollars ($25,000) on real property that is owned by the individual and used by the individual as a principal place of residence.	

State	Description of Property and Amount	Applicability of Federal Exemptions
Texas	Homestead: Unlimited dollar amount **Tex. Const. Art. XVI § 51 (2010). Amount of Homestead; Uses** The homestead, not in a town or city, shall consist of not more than two hundred acres of land, which may be in one or more parcels, with the improvements thereon; the homestead in a city, town or village, shall consist of lot or contiguous lots amounting to not more than 10 acres of land, together with any improvements on the land; provided, that the homestead in a city, town or village shall be used for the purposes of a home, or as both an urban home and a place to exercise a calling or business, of the homestead claimant, whether a single adult person, or the head of a family; provided also, that any temporary renting of the homestead shall not change the character of the same, when no other homestead has been acquired; provided further that a release or refinance of an existing lien against a homestead as to a part of the homestead does not create an additional burden on the part of the homestead property that is unreleased or subject to the refinance, and a new lien is not invalid only for that reason. **Tex. Prop. Code Ann. § 41.002 (2010) § 41.002. Definition of Homestead** (a) If used for the purposes of an urban home or as both an urban home and a place to exercise a calling or business, the homestead of a family or a single, adult person, not otherwise entitled to a homestead, shall consist of not more	No statutory prohibition. Use of federal exemptions permitted.

Table 1. (Continued)

State	Description of Property and Amount	Applicability of Federal Exemptions
	than 10 acres of land which may be in one or more contiguous lots, together with any improvements thereon. (b) If used for the purposes of a rural home, the homestead shall consist of: (1) for a family, not more than 200 acres, which may be in one or more parcels, with the improvements thereon; or (2) for a single, adult person, not otherwise entitled to a homestead, not more than 100 acres, which may be in one or more parcels, with the improvements thereon. (c) A homestead is considered to be urban if, at the time the designation is made, the property is: (1) located within the limits of a municipality or its extraterritorial jurisdiction or a platted subdivision; and (2) served by police protection, paid or volunteer fire protection, and at least three of the following services provided by a municipality or under contract to a municipality: (A) electric; (B) natural gas; (C) sewer; (D) storm sewer; and (E) water. (d) The definition of a homestead as provided in this section applies to all homesteads in this state whenever created.	

State	Description of Property and Amount	Applicability of Federal Exemptions
Utah	Homestead: $20,000 if primary personal residence; $40,000 jointly owned; $5,000 if *not* primary personal residence; $10,000 if jointly owned **Utah Code Ann. § 78B-5-503 (2011). Homestead exemption—Definitions—Excepted obligations— Water rights and interests—Conveyance—Sale and disposition—Property right for federal tax purposes** (1) For purposes of this section: (c) "Primary personal residence" means a dwelling or mobile home, and the land surrounding it, not exceeding one acre, as is reasonably necessary for the use of the dwelling or mobile home, in which the individual and the individual's household reside. … (2) (a) An individual is entitled to a homestead exemption consisting of property in this state in an amount not exceeding: (i) $5,000 in value if the property consists in whole or in part of property which is not the primary personal residence of the individual; or (ii) $20,000 in value if the property claimed is the primary personal residence of the individual. (b) If the property claimed as exempt is jointly owned, each joint owner is entitled to a homestead exemption; however (i) for property exempt under Subsection (2)(a)(i), the maximum exemption may not exceed $10,000 per	Federal exemptions *not* permitted. **Utah Code Ann. § 78B-5-513 (2011). Exemption provisions applicable in bankruptcy proceedings** No individual may exempt from the property of the estate in any bankruptcy proceeding the property specified in Subsection (d) of Section 522 of the Bankruptcy Reform Act (P.L. 95-598), except as expressly permitted under this part.

Table 1. (Continued)

State	Description of Property and Amount	Applicability of Federal Exemptions
	household; or (ii) for property exempt under Subsection (2)(a)(ii), the maximum exemption may not exceed $40,000 per household. (c) A person may claim a homestead exemption in either or both of the following: (i) one or more parcels of real property together with appurtenances and improvements; or (ii) a mobile home in which the claimant resides.	
Vermont	Homestead: $125,000 **Vt. Stat. Ann. tit. 27 § 101 (2011). Definition; exemption from attachment and execution** The homestead of a natural person consisting of a dwelling house, outbuildings and the land used in connection therewith, not exceeding $125,000.00 in value, and owned and used or kept by such person as a homestead together with the rents, issues, profits, and products thereof, shall be exempt from attachment and execution except as hereinafter provided.	No statutory prohibition. Use of federal exemptions permitted.
Virginia	No specific homestead exemption. Wildcard: $5,000 ($10,000 if a least 65 years old), plus $500 per dependant; $10,000 added for veterans with at least 40% service connected disability	Federal exemptions *not* permitted. **Va. Code Ann. § 34-3.1 (2011).** **Property specified in Bankruptcy Reform Act not exempt**

State	Description of Property and Amount	Applicability of Federal Exemptions
	Va. Code Ann. § 34-4 (2011). Exemption created Every householder shall be entitled, in addition to the property or estate exempt under §§ 23-38.81, 34-26, 34-27, 34-29, and 64.1-151.3, to hold exempt from creditor process arising out of a debt, real and personal property, or either, to be selected by the householder, including money and debts due the householder not exceeding $5,000 in value or, if the householder is 65 years of age or older, not exceeding $10,000 in value. In addition, upon a showing that a householder supports dependents, the householder shall be entitled to hold exempt from creditor process real and personal property, or either, selected by the householder, including money or monetary obligations or liabilities due the householder, not exceeding $500 in value for each dependent. For the purposes of this section, "dependent" means an individual who derives support primarily from the householder and who does not have assets sufficient to support himself, but in no case shall an individual be the dependent of more than one householder. **Va. Code. Ann. §34-4.1 (2011). Additional exemption for certain veterans** Every veteran residing in this Commonwealth having a service connected disability of forty percent or more, as rated by the Veterans Administration of the United States, shall be entitled, in addition to the property or	No individual may exempt from the property of the estate in any bankruptcy proceeding the property specified in subsection (d) of § 522 of the Bankruptcy Reform Act (P.L. 95-598), except as may otherwise be expressly permitted under this title.

Table 1. (Continued)

State	Description of Property and Amount	Applicability of Federal Exemptions
	estate which he is entitled to hold exempt from creditor process under §§ 34-4, 34-26, 34-27, 34-29, and 64.1-151.3, to hold exempt from creditor process his real and personal property, or either, to be selected by him by the writings required by §§ 34-6 and 34-14, including money and debts due him, not exceeding $10,000 in value.	
Washington	Homestead: $125,000; unlimited in limited circumstances in which income taxes are owed to another state on retirement benefits received while a resident of the state of Washington[f] **Wash. Rev. Code Ann. § 6.13.030 (2011). Homestead exemption limited** A homestead may consist of lands, as described in RCW 6.13.010, regardless of area, but the homestead exemption amount shall not exceed the lesser of (1) the total net value of the lands, manufactured homes, mobile home, improvements, and other personal property, as described in RCW 6.13.010, or (2) the sum of one hundred twenty-five thousand dollars in the case of lands, manufactured homes, mobile home, and improvements, or the sum of fifteen thousand dollars in the case of other personal property described in RCW 6.13.010, except where the homestead is subject to execution, attachment, or seizure by or under any legal process whatever to satisfy a judgment in favor of any state for failure to pay that state's income tax on benefits	No statutory prohibition. Use of federal exemptions permitted.

State	Description of Property and Amount	Applicability of Federal Exemptions
	received while a resident of the state of Washington from a pension or other retirement plan, in which event there shall be no dollar limit on the value of the exemption.	
West Virginia	Homestead: $25,000 generally; $250,000 if a physician filing due in part to malpractice verdict or judgment and has $1 million (per occurrence) malpractice insurance **W. Va. Code § 38-9-1 (2011). Persons entitled to homestead; value** Any husband, wife, parent or other head of a household residing in this State, or the infant children of deceased or insane parents, owning a homestead shall by operation of law have a homestead exemption therein to the value of five thousand dollars, subject to the provisions of section 48, article VI of the Constitution of this State. **W. Va. Code § 38-9-2 (2011). Definitions** As used in this article: (1) "Homestead" means property owned and used as the principal home for the debtor, his spouse or a dependent, or any or all of them, whether classified as real property, chattel real, a fixture or personal property; **W. Va. Code § 38-10-4 (2011). Exemptions of property in bankruptcy proceedings** (a) The debtor's interest, not to exceed twenty-five thousand dollars in value, in real property or personal property that the debtor or a dependent of the debtor uses as a residence, in a cooperative that owns property	Federal exemptions *not* permitted. **W. Va. Code § 38-10-4 (2011). Exemptions of property in bankruptcy proceedings** Pursuant to the provisions of 11 U. S. C. § 522(b) (1), this state specifically does not authorize debtors who are domiciled in this state to exempt the property specified under the provisions of 11 U. S. C. § 522(d). …

Table 1. (Continued)

State	Description of Property and Amount	Applicability of Federal Exemptions
	that the debtor or a dependent of the debtor uses as a residence or in a burial plot for the debtor or a dependent of the debtor: Provided, That when the debtor is a physician licensed to practice medicine in this state under article three §§ 30-3-1 et seq. or article fourteen §§ 30-14-1 et seq., chapter thirty of this code, and has commenced a bankruptcy proceeding in part due to a verdict or judgment entered in a medical professional liability action, if the physician has current medical malpractice insurance in the amount of at least one million dollars for each occurrence, the debtor physician's interest that is exempt under this subsection may exceed twenty-five thousand dollars in value but may not exceed two hundred fifty thousand dollars per household.	
Wisconsin	Homestead: $75,000 **Wis. Stat. § 815.20 (2011). Homestead exemption definition** (1) An exempt homestead as defined in s. 990.01 (14) selected by a resident owner and occupied by him or her shall be exempt from execution, from the lien of every judgment and from liability for the debts of the owner to the amount of 75,000, except mortgages, laborers, mechanics and purchase money liens and taxes and except as otherwise provided. The exemption shall not be impaired by temporary removal with the intention to	No statutory prohibition. Use of federal exemptions permitted.

State	Description of Property and Amount	Applicability of Federal Exemptions
	reoccupy the premises as a homestead nor by the sale of the homestead, but shall extend to the proceeds derived from the sale to an amount not exceeding 75,000, while held, with the intention to procure another homestead with the proceeds, for 2 years. The exemption extends to land owned by husband and wife jointly or in common or as marital property, and each spouse may claim a homestead exemption of not more than 75,000. The exemption extends to the interest therein of tenants in common, having a homestead thereon with the consent of the cotenants, and oto any estate less than a fee. (2) Any owner of an exempt homestead against whom a judgment has been rendered and entered in the judgment and lien docket, and any heir, devisee or grantee of the owner, or any mortgagee of the homestead, may proceed under s. 806.04 for declaratory relief if the homestead is less than 75,000 in value and the owner of the judgment shall fail, for 10 days after demand, to execute a recordable release of the homestead from the judgment owners judgment lien.	
Wyoming	Homestead: $10,000 generally; $6,000 if mobile home **Wyo. Stat. Ann. § 1-20-101 (2011). Homestead exemption; right and amount** Every resident of the state is entitled to a homestead not exceeding ten thousand dollars ($10,000.00) in value, exe-mpt from execution and attachment arising from any debt,	Federal exemptions *not* permitted. **Wyo. Stat. Ann. § 1-20-109 (2011). Exemptions from estates in bankruptcy** In accordance with 11 U.S.C. § 522(b)(1), the exemptions from property of the estate in bankruptcy provided in 11 U.S.C. §

Table 1. (Continued)

State	Description of Property and Amount	Applicability of Federal Exemptions
	contract or civil obligation entered into or incurred. **Wyo. Stat. Ann. § 1-20-104 (2011). Homestead exemption; composition** The homestead may consist of a house and lot or lots in any town or city, or a farm consisting of any number of acres, or a house trailer or other movable home, whether or not equipped with wheels or resting upon immovable support, the value of which does not exceed six thousand dollars ($6,000.00).	522(d) are not authorized in cases where Wyoming law is applicable on the date of the filing of the petition and the debtor's domicile has been located in Wyoming for the one hundred eighty (180) days immediately preceding the date of the filing of the petition or for a longer portion of the one hundred eighty (180) day period than in any other place.

Source: Table compiled by the Congressional Research Service using statutory information available on the Westlaw and Lexis databases as well as other publicly available resources.

a. *See* In re Tinkess, 9 Alaska B.R. 33, 39-46 (Bankr. D. Alaska 2008) (holding that Alaska has not opted out of federal exemptions and Alaska's debtors may use either state exemptions or those in 11 U.S.C. § 522(d)).

b. On June 2, 2011, § 4426 was amended to change "522(b)(2)(A)" to read "522(b)(3)(A)" so as to incorporate redesignation by BAPCPA in 2005. 2011 Me. Laws 203.

c. Mass. Acts, Chap. 395, § 3. Available at http://www.malegislature.gov/Laws/ SessionLaws/Acts/2010/ Chapter395.

d. Adjustments that took effect on April 1, 2010 are available at http://www. ohiojudges.org/index.cfm.

e. This statute was amended with an effective date of July 29, 2011; however, the subsections cited here were not changed.

f. For a number of years, California broadly asserted that retirement benefits received by those who were not currently residents of California were nonetheless subject to income tax in California to the extent that the right to the benefits was earned by the taxpayer while resident in California.

SCOPE OF THE SURVEY OF HOMESTEAD EXEMPTIONS

State laws were reviewed on both the Westlaw and LEXIS computer databases. In the table, the entry for each state first provides a brief synopsis of the homestead exemption available to debtors in bankruptcy as well as the extent to which debtors may elect to use federal rather than state exemptions. In some cases, *de minimis* "wildcard" exemptions that may be used for either real or personal property are noted, but the survey is not comprehensive with respect to them. They are more likely to be noted when a state has an extremely limited homestead exemption. Relevant excerpts of the state's statutory language is provided after the synopsis. Except as it is included in the excerpted statutory language, the survey does not address whether there is an exemption for proceeds after the sale of a homestead, nor does it address exemptions established by case law for homesteads held as tenancies by the entirety. Except as noted, state law provisions that constitute *exceptions* to the homestead exemption are not included in the survey.

End Notes

[1] 11 U.S.C.A. § 522(d)(1) (West Supp. 2011). The amount as enacted was $18,450, but it is adjusted periodically by Judicial Conference of the United States. $21,625 is the amount for cases filed on or after April 1, 2010. 75 Fed. Reg. 8747 (Feb. 25, 2010). *See* Adjustment of Dollar Amounts, 11 U.S.C.A. § 104 (West Supp. 2011).

[2] 11 U.S.C.A. § 522(d)(5) (West Supp. 2011). The amount as enacted was $975, but it is adjusted periodically by Judicial Conference of the United States. $1,150 is the amount for cases filed on or after April 1, 2010. 75 Fed. Reg. 8747 (Feb. 25, 2010). *See* Adjustment of Dollar Amounts, 11 U.S.C.A. § 104 (West Supp. 2011).

[3] 11 U.S.C. § 522(b)(1).

[4] Some states restrict the use of state exemptions to residents of the state. If such a state has "opted out" of the federal exemptions, the federal exemptions will, nonetheless, be available to those who are subject to that state's laws as a result of 11 U.S.C. § 522(b)(3)(A) but are prohibited from using the state exemptions under state law.

[5] 11 U.S.C. § 522(b)(2).

[6] As enacted, the exemption amount was $125,000; however, this amount is adjusted periodically by Judicial Conference of the United States. Effective for cases filed on or after April 1, 2010, this amount is $146,450. 75 Fed. Reg. 8747 (Feb. 25, 2010). *See* Adjustment of Dollar Amounts, 11 U.S.C.A. § 104 (West Supp. 2011).

[7] 11 U.S.C. §101 *et seq.*

[8] 11 U.S.C.A. § 522(p) (West Supp. 2011).

[9] 11 U.S.C. § 522(q)(1)(A).

[10] 11 U.S.C. § 522(q)(1)(B).

[11] 11 U.S.C. § 522(o).

[12] The code specifies "730 days." 11 U.S.C. § 522(b)(3)(A).

In: Bankruptcy Exemptions
Editors: R. Rhodes and P. J. Lambert
ISBN: 978-1-61942-381-7

Chapter 2

EXEMPTIONS FOR FIREARMS IN BANKRUPTCY

Carol A. Pettit and Vastine D. Platte

SUMMARY

The U.S. Supreme Court's decisions regarding the nature of the people's right to "keep and bear arms," as guaranteed in the Second Amendment to the U.S. Constitution, has focused some interest on the extent to which firearms are protected from the reach of creditors under either federal or state laws. State laws protecting certain property from creditors' claims may be used both in and outside of the bankruptcy context. Federal law may also protect certain property from creditors' claims in bankruptcy.

Although a number of states have provisions explicitly shielding firearms from the claims of creditors, there is currently no such provision in the U.S. Bankruptcy Code (title 11). In the 111th Congress, legislation was passed in the House (H.R. 5827) that would have provided an explicit federal exemption in bankruptcy for a debtor's aggregate interest, up to $3,000, "in a single rifle, shotgun, or pistol, or any combination thereof." The bill also included the means for protecting firearms by including them—subject to the same value and type restrictions—in the definition of "household goods" for which nonpossessory, nonpurchase-money security interest liens could be avoided in bankruptcy. Similar legislation has been introduced in the 112th Congress: the Protecting Gun Owners in Bankruptcy Act of 2011 (H.R. 1181).

The Bankruptcy Code generally provides two options for claiming exemptions in bankruptcy—either the exemptions provided in 11 U.S.C. § 522(d) or the exemptions available under state law. However, debtors may only choose to use the federal exemptions in § 522(d) if their state specifically authorizes them to do so. Because the proposed federal exemption for firearms would be included in § 522(d), debtors whose states do not authorize them to use the § 522(d) exemptions would not benefit from the proposed change in exemptions. They might, however, benefit from the inclusion of firearms in the definition of household goods, because they could then have the option of freeing those firearms from liens that were based on a nonpossessory, nonpurchase-money security interest.

There is great variety in the extent of the protection from creditors the states provide for firearms. The majority of states provide no explicit protection. Among those that provide protection (17 states plus Puerto Rico and the District of Columbia), the conditions for providing that protection vary. Some states limit the exemption by both the number and value of the firearms; some do not limit the number but may limit either the value of each firearm or the aggregate value of all. Other states specify the type of firearms that can be exempted. In most states that allow an exemption for firearms, the exemption is not dependent upon the way in which the firearm is used. Several states, however, exempt only guns that are for personal use, and one state requires that the firearm be used for business purposes.

The U.S. Supreme Court's decisions regarding the nature of the people's right to "keep and bear arms," as guaranteed in the Second Amendment to the U.S. Constitution,[1] has focused some interest in the extent to which firearms are protected from the reach of creditors under either federal or state laws.[2] State laws that protect certain property from creditors' claims generally are designed to apply in non-bankruptcy contexts, but may also be used in bankruptcy. Federal law also protects certain property from creditors' claims in bankruptcy. Additionally, a debtor in bankruptcy may be able to avoid liens against exempt property if a lien impairs the exemption and is either a judicial lien or a nonpossessory, nonpurchase-money security interest.

Recently introduced legislation,[3] similar to legislation passed by the House in the 111th Congress,[4] would allow a specific federal exemption for firearms and would include firearms in the definition of household goods whose exemptions could be protected from impairment by liens. A number of states provide their own exemptions for firearms. The provisions of these states are provided in **Table 1**.

FEDERAL EXEMPTIONS UNDER THE U.S. BANKRUPTCY CODE

Section 522 of the U.S. Bankruptcy Code[5] addresses the extent to which an individual debtor may elect to exempt equity in certain property from becoming part of the bankruptcy estate. Property exempted from the bankruptcy estate is not available to satisfy creditors. Among the exemptions explicitly provided in the Bankruptcy Code—the federal exemptions—are a homestead exemption in the amount of $20,200,[6] a vehicle exemption in the amount of $3,225,[7] and exemptions for jewelry,[8] tools of the trade,[9] and household goods.[10] There is also a "wildcard" exemption of $1,075[11] that can also be applied to any property so long as the federal exemptions are available to the debtor.

To the extent allowed under state law, the Bankruptcy Code permits debtors to choose between using the federal exemptions or those available under applicable state law.[12] This is an "either/or" choice—debtors are not allowed to choose to use some state exemptions and some federal exemptions.[13] When a petition is filed jointly by husband and wife or when the individual cases of a husband and wife are ordered to be jointly administered, each spouse must choose the same set of exemptions.[14] However, debtors in many states have no choice to make because their state law prohibits the use of the federal exemptions.[15] These federal exemptions are available to debtors *only* to the extent they are not prohibited by the applicable state.[16] Puerto Rico, the District of Columbia, and 17 states[17] allow debtors to choose between federal and state exemptions.

STATES' EXEMPTIONS FOR FIREARMS

The conditions for exempting firearms vary among the relevant states. Some states specify the number of firearms that may be exempted without regard to the value of the firearms.[18] Other states limit the exemption to one firearm and further limit the claimed exemption by either the value of the firearm[19] or the aggregate value of the statutorily exempt property in which the firearm is included.[20] Oregon allows an exemption for one pistol as well as one rifle or shotgun, but limits the total exemption value of the two firearms to no more than $1,000.[21] Several states put no limit on the number of firearms that may be exempted so long as the total value of the firearms, when aggregated with the value of certain other property is less than a specific amount.[22] In these states, there is generally a limit to the value of each firearm. One state, Oklahoma, allows an unlimited number of firearms to be exempted so long as the total value of the firearms, alone, is no more than $2,000.[23]

In most of the states, the exemption is not controlled by the way in which the firearm is used. Several states, however, exempt only guns that are for personal use. Three of these specify that the firearms are to be "held primarily for the personal, family, or household use of [the debtor]."[24] Oregon law specifies that the firearms must be "for the own use and defense of the citizen."[25] Only one state, Louisiana, requires that the exempted firearm be used for business purposes.[26] Both Montana and Nevada exempt "all arms ... required by law to be kept by any person"[27] in addition to the one gun, selected by the debtor, that each allows.

PROPOSED LEGISLATION

H.R. 1181, the Protecting Gun Owners in Bankruptcy Act of 2011, was introduced on March 17, 2011, in the 112th Congress. The bill parallels an earlier bill[28] passed by the House in the 111th Congress, but not voted on by the Senate. The bill would provide a firearms exemption that could be used in bankruptcy by a debtor who opted to use federal rather than state exemptions and was allowed to do so by the relevant state's law.

The bill would amend § 522(d) of the Bankruptcy Code to add an exemption for the debtor's aggregate interest—up to a total value of $3,000—"in a single rifle, shotgun, or pistol or any combination thereof."[29] The addition of this exemption would not reduce the amount allowed for any other type of exemption under § 522.

Additionally, the bill would amend § 522(f)(4)(A) to include firearms in the definition of "household goods." As with the exemption for firearms, this provision would apply to any number or combination of rifles, shotguns, and pistols so long as the aggregate value was no more than $3,000. Inclusion of firearms in the definition of household goods would not increase the exemption available for firearms, but it would allow debtors to avoid liens that are nonpossessory, nonpurchase-money security interests on those firearms, under § 522(f)(1)(B), as they are currently able to avoid such liens on other household goods. The bill would not change the maximum value of household goods whose liens could be avoided in bankruptcy.

Table 1. State Exemptions for Firearms

State	Statutory Text
Arizona	**Ariz. Rev. Stat. § 33-1125 (2011). Personal items.** The following property of a debtor used primarily for personal, family or household purposes shall be exempt from process: 7. One typewriter, one bicycle, one sewing machine, a family bible, a lot in any burial ground, one shotgun or one rifle or one pistol, not in excess of an aggregate fair market value of five hundred dollars.
Idaho	**Idaho Code Ann. § 11-605 (2011). Exemptions of personal property and disposable earnings subject to value limitations.** (8) An individual is entitled to exemption of one (1) firearm valued at less than seven hundred fifty dollars ($750), or less.
Iowa	**Iowa Code § 627.6 (2010). General exemptions.** A debtor who is a resident of this state may hold exempt from execution the following property: 2. One shotgun, and either one rifle or one musket.
Louisiana	**La. Rev. Stat. Ann. § 13:3881 (2011). General exemptions from seizure.** A. The following income or property of a debtor is exempt from seizure under any writ, mandate, or process whatsoever, except as otherwise herein provided: (2) That property necessary to the exercise of a trade, calling, or profession by which he earns his livelihood, which shall be limited to the following: (e) One firearm with a maximum value of five hundred dollars.
Mississippi	**Miss. Code Ann. § 85-3-1 (2010). Property exempt from seizure under execution or attachment.** There shall be exempt from seizure under execution or attachment: (a) Tangible personal property of the following kinds selected by the debtor, not exceeding Ten Thousand Dollars ($10,000.00) in cumulative value: (i) Household goods, wearing apparel, books, animals or crops; Household goods, as used in this paragraph (a), means clothing, furniture, appliances, one (1) radio and one (1) television, one (1) firearm, one (1) lawnmower, linens, china, crockery, kitchenware, and personal effects (including wedding rings) of the debtor and his dependents; however, works of art, electronic entertainment equipment (except one (1) television and one (1)

Table 1. (Continued)

State	Statutory Text
	radio), jewelry (other than wedding rings), and items acquired as antiques are not included within the scope of the term "household goods." This paragraph (a) shall not apply to distress warrants issued for collection of taxes due the state or to wages described in Section 85-3-4.
Montana	**Mont. Code Ann. § 25-13-609 (2010). Personal property exempt subject to value limitations.** A judgment debtor is entitled to exemption from execution of the following: (1) the judgment debtor's interest, not to exceed \$4,500 in aggregate value, to the extent of a value not exceeding \$600 in any item of property, in household furnishings and goods, appliances, jewelry, wearing apparel, books, firearms and other sporting goods, animals, feed, crops, and musical instruments; **Mont. Code Ann. § 25-13-613 (2010). Property necessary to carry out governmental functions.** (1) In addition to the property mentioned in 25-13-609(1), the following property is exempt from all judgment debtors: (b) all arms, uniforms, and accouterments required by law to be kept by any person and one gun to be selected by the debtor.
Nevada	**Nev. Rev. Stat. Ann. § 21.090 (2011). Property exempt from execution.** 1. The following property is exempt from execution, except as otherwise specifically provided in this section or required by federal law: (i) All arms, uniforms and accouterments required by law to be kept by any person, and also one gun, to be selected by the debtor.
Ohio	**Ohio Rev. Code Ann. § 2329.66 (2011). Exempted interests and rights.** (A) Every person who is domiciled in this state may hold property exempt from execution, garnishment, attachment, or sale to satisfy a judgment or order, as follows: (4) (a) The person's interest, not to exceed five hundred twenty-five dollars in any particular item or ten thousand seven hundred seventy-five dollars in aggregate value, in household furnishings, household goods, wearing apparel, appliances, books, animals, crops, musical instruments, firearms, and hunting and fishing equipment that are held primarily for the personal, family, or household use of the person.

State	Statutory Text
Oklahoma	**Okla. Stat. tit. 31, § 1 (2011). Property exempt from attachment, execution or other forced sale—Bankruptcy proceedings.** A. Except as otherwise provided in this title and notwithstanding subsection B of this section, the following property shall be reserved to every person residing in the state, exempt from attachment or execution and every other species of forced sale for the payment of debts, except as herein provided: 14. Guns, not to exceed Two Thousand Dollars ($2,000.00) in aggregate value, that are held primarily for the personal, family or household use of such person or a dependent of such person, provided that nothing in this subsection shall be construed to allow a person to exempt guns which are used mainly as an investment or nonpersonal, family or household use.
Oregon	**Or. Rev. Stat. § 18.362 (2010). Exemption for firearms.** Every citizen of this state above the age of 16 years shall be entitled to have, hold and keep, for the own use and defense of the citizen and shall have exempt from execution one rifle or shotgun and one pistol. The combined value of all firearms claimed as exempt under this section may not exceed $1,000.
Texas	**Tex. Prop. Code Ann. § 42.002 (2010). Personal Property.** (a) The following personal property is exempt under Section 42.001(a): (7) two firearms.
Wisconsin	**Wis. Stat. § 815.18 (2011). Property exempt from execution.** (3) Exempt property. The debtors interest in or right to receive the following property is exempt, except as specifically provided in this section and ss. 70.20 (2), 71.91 (5m) and (6), 74.55 (2) and 102.28 (5): (d) Consumer goods. Household goods and furnishings, wearing apparel, keepsakes, jewelry and other articles of personal adornment, appliances, books, musical instruments, firearms, sporting goods, animals, or other tangible personal property held primarily for the personal, family or household use of the debtor or a dependent of the debtor, not to exceed $12,000 in aggregate value.

Source: LexisNexis State Codes Database.

End Notes

[1] District of Columbia v. Heller, 554 U.S. 570; 128 S. Ct. 2783 (2008); McDonald v. Chicago, 561 U.S. ___; 130 S. Ct. 3020 (2010). For additional information on these cases, see CRS

Report R41750, *The Second Amendment: An Overview of District of Columbia v. Heller and McDonald v. City of Chicago*, by Vivian S. Chu. For information about gun control legislation, see CRS Report RL32842, *Gun Control Legislation*, by William J. Krouse. Please note that discussion of any possible constitutional issues involving firearms and bankruptcy is beyond the scope of this report.

2 The U.S. Constitution gives Congress the right to make uniform laws concerning bankruptcy. Art. 1, § 8, cl. 4.

3 H.R. 1181 (112th Congress).

4 H.R. 5827 (111th Congress).

5 11 U.S.C. § 101 *et seq.*

6 11 U.S.C.A. § 522(d)(1) (West Supp. 2009). The amount as enacted was $18,450, but it is adjusted periodically by the Judicial Conference of the United States. $20,200 is the amount for cases filed on or after April 1, 2007. 72 Fed. Reg. 7082 (Feb. 14, 2007). *See* Adjustment of Dollar Amounts, 11 U.S.C.A. § 104 (West Supp. 2009).

7 11 U.S.C.A. § 522(d)(2) (West Supp. 2009). This amount is adjusted periodically by the Judicial Conference of the United States.

8 11 U.S.C.A. § 522(d)(4) (West Supp. 2009).

9 11 U.S.C.A. § 522(d)(6) (West Supp. 2009).

10 11 U.S.C.A. § 522(d)(3) (West Supp. 2009).

11 11 U.S.C.A. § 522(d)(5) (West Supp. 2009). The amount as enacted was $975, but it is adjusted periodically by Judicial Conference of the United States. $1,075 is the amount for cases filed on or after April 1, 2007. 72 Fed. Reg. 7082 (Feb. 14, 2007). *See* Adjustment of Dollar Amounts, 11 U.S.C.A. § 104 (West Supp. 2009).

12 11 U.S.C. § 522(b)(1)-(2).

13 However, when a debtor uses the exemptions available under state law, an exemption for many retirement funds, as well as some property owned in tenancy by the entirety or joint tenancy, is also available even if not provided under state law. 11 U.S.C. § 522(d)(3)(B)-(C).

14 11 U.S.C. § 522(b)(1).

15 For a table of states' provisions restricting a debtor's use of federal exemptions, see CRS Report R40891, *Homestead Exemptions in Bankruptcy After the Bankruptcy Abuse Prevention and Consumer Protection Act of 2005 (BAPCPA)*, by Carol A. Pettit and Julia Taylor.

16 11 U.S.C. § 522(b)(2). In applying this provision, the District of Columbia and Puerto Rico are each treated as states. 11 U.S.C. § 101(52).

17 Alaska, Arkansas, Connecticut, Hawaii, Kentucky, Massachusetts, Michigan, Minnesota, New Hampshire, New Jersey, New Mexico, Pennsylvania, Rhode Island, Texas, Vermont, Washington, and Wisconsin.

18 Mont. Code Ann. § 25-13-613(1)(b); Nev. Rev. Stat. Ann. § 21.090(1)(i); Tex. Prop. Code Ann. § 42.002(a)(7).

19 Idaho Code Ann. § 11-605(7) (2009); La. Rev. Stat. Ann. § 13.3881(A)(2)(e) (2009).

20 Miss. Code Ann. § 85-6-1(a) (2009).

21 Or. Rev. Stat. § 18.362 (2007).

22 Mont. Code Ann. § 25-13-609(1) (2009) (explicitly allowing exemption of firearms in addition to the one exempted under § 25-13-613(1)(b)); Ohio Rev. Code Ann. §2329.66 (2010); Wis. Stat. § 815.18 (2009).

23 Okla. Stat. tit. 31, § 1(a)(14) (2009).

24 Ohio Rev. Code Ann. § 2329.66(A)(4)(a); Okla.Stat. tit. 31, § 1(A)(14); Wis. Stat. § 815.18(3)(d).

25 Or. Rev. Stat. § 18.362.

26 La. Rev. Stat. Ann. § 13:3881(A)(2)(e) (2009) ("property necessary to the exercise of a trade, calling, or profession by which [the debtor] earns his livelihood").

27 Mont. Code Ann. § 25-13-613(1)(b); Nev. Rev. Stat. Ann. § 21.090(1)(i).

[28] H.R. 5827 (111th Congress). The bill reported out of committee and passed by the House differed from the introduced version of the bill, which would have exempted a single rifle, shotgun, or pistol of any value, but which would have limited the aggregate value of multiple firearms to $1,500.

[29] H.R. 1181 § 2 (adding 11 U.S.C. § 522(d)(13)).

Chapter Sources

Chapter 1 - This is an edited, reformatted and augmented version of a Congressional Research Service publication, R40891, dated August 25, 2011.

Chapter 2 - This is an edited, reformatted and augmented version of a Congressional Research Service publication, R41799, dated May 2, 2011.

INDEX

A

adjustment, 50
administrators, 8, 58
age, 2, 7, 11, 20, 29, 37, 39, 52, 60, 61, 72, 74, 76, 81, 95
Alaska, 6, 86, 96
alienation, 55
assessment, 54
assets, 4, 81
attachment, 7, 14, 16, 20, 21, 23, 26, 28, 31, 33, 39, 40, 51, 52, 53, 58, 62, 64, 67, 68, 69, 70, 75, 80, 82, 85, 93, 94, 95
authority, 9, 18

B

bankruptcy, vii, 1, 2, 3, 4, 7, 9, 12, 14, 15, 16, 17, 19, 21, 24, 25, 26, 28, 30, 32, 49, 50, 52, 53, 54, 61, 63, 64, 66, 70, 75, 79, 81, 83, 84, 85
base, 73
beneficiaries, 35, 36
benefits, 2, 35, 36, 38, 52, 82, 86
bible, 93
bonds, 56
Bureau of Labor Statistics, 70

C

case law, 87
cash, 14, 31, 67
Chicago, 95
children, 2, 5, 9, 34, 41, 48, 63, 68, 69, 75, 76, 83
citizens, 75
City, 96
classes, 2
clothing, 93
coaches, 15
commerce, 49
commercial, 65
common law, 60
community, 11, 12, 56
composition, 86
computer, 87
consent, 17, 25, 55, 85
Constitution, vii, 8, 17, 51, 54, 66, 72, 73, 83, 89, 90, 96
constitutional issues, 96
construction, 52
consumer price index, 64
Consumer Price Index, 70, 71
consumers, 64
creditors, vii, 1, 3, 23, 44, 60, 89, 90, 91
crops, 93, 94

D

debtors, vii, 1, 2, 3, 4, 23, 24, 49, 59, 62, 66, 83, 86, 87, 90, 91, 92, 94, 95
debts, 5, 23, 27, 33, 40, 48, 64, 66, 68, 81, 82, 84, 95
Department of Labor, 70
destruction, 10
disability, 2, 11, 29, 37, 45, 80, 81
disaster, 28
disposition, 79
distress, 94
District of Columbia, vii, 1, 2, 3, 16, 17, 90, 91, 95, 96

E

earnings, 93
employment, 11, 29
enforcement, 60, 63
equipment, 93, 94
equity, 2, 3, 4, 16, 56, 57, 91
evidence, 45, 54
exercise, 77, 93, 96

F

faith, 24
family members, 37, 42
federal law, 5, 25, 26, 27, 52, 55, 57, 94
financial, 56, 69
firearms, vii, 89, 90, 91, 92, 94, 95, 96, 97
fishing, 94
force, 47
foreclosure, 58
fraud, 4, 34
funds, 56, 96

G

Georgia, 18, 19
gun control, 96

H

Hawaii, 20, 96
health, 28, 62
health care, 28, 62
homes, 15, 39, 43, 46, 73, 82
House, 89, 90, 92, 97
housing, 37
human, 68
hunting, 94
husband, 3, 5, 12, 13, 25, 32, 34, 49, 50, 52, 55, 56, 69, 83, 85, 91

I

improvements, 5, 8, 17, 18, 22, 25, 26, 51, 55, 62, 65, 77, 78, 80, 82
income, 2, 5, 11, 27, 28, 82, 86, 93
income tax, 2, 28, 82, 86
individuals, 23, 37, 49, 51, 60, 75
insane, 83
insurance policy, 28
investment, 95
Iowa, 2, 24, 93
issues, 2, 53, 80

J

Judicial Conference of the United States, 87, 96
jurisdiction, 18, 34, 78

L

laws, vii, 1, 2, 4, 5, 7, 8, 18, 22, 23, 27, 33, 48, 55, 63, 68, 74, 87, 89, 90, 96
legislation, 89, 90, 96
Louisiana, 2, 27, 92, 93

M

majority, 2, 90
manufactured housing, 21, 51, 57
marital status, 2, 39, 40
Maryland, 30
matter, iv
medical, 2, 69, 84
medical assistance, 69
medicine, 45, 84
mental impairment, 37
Mexico, 58, 96
Missouri, 52
Montana, 53, 92, 94

N

natural gas, 78
NRS, 55, 56, 57

O

Oklahoma, 2, 64, 92, 95
ownership, 4, 20, 23, 33, 35, 39, 40

P

parents, 9, 83
police, 78
policy, 38
preparation, iv
prima facie, 54
protection, vii, 1, 3, 7, 39, 40, 44, 78, 90
Puerto Rico, 90, 91, 96

R

radio, 93, 94
real estate, 24
real property, 2, 7, 13, 15, 16, 17, 19, 20, 21, 31, 32, 39, 51, 52, 53, 54, 60, 62, 67, 70, 73, 75, 76, 80, 83
recommendations, iv
reconciliation, 21
Reform, 15, 16, 18, 25, 51, 61, 62, 64, 75, 79, 80, 81
relief, 52, 85
rent, 34, 46, 47, 68
repair, 17, 28
requirements, 11, 37, 45, 47
resources, 86
response, 2
restrictions, 2, 89
retirement, 2, 82, 83, 86, 96
rings, 93, 94
rules, 67

S

scope, 94, 96
securities, 4, 67
security, 11, 89, 90, 92
seizure, 16, 27, 28, 39, 40, 51, 82, 93
Senate, 92
showing, 81
sibling, 32
Social Security, 11, 45
Social Security Administration, 45
South Dakota, 2, 72, 73
species, 64, 95
state laws, vii, 89, 90
states, vii, 1, 2, 3, 4, 87, 89, 90, 91, 92, 96
statutes, 7, 14, 31, 32, 51, 54, 64, 73
stock, 20, 58, 59, 60
Supreme Court, vii, 89, 90

T

taxation, 60
taxes, 8, 17, 18, 25, 33, 51, 52, 55, 60, 61, 68, 72, 84, 94
tenants, 23, 24, 35, 36, 44, 85
terminal illness, 28
time constraints, 30
Title I, 11

Title II, 11
trade, 91, 93, 96

U

U.S. Department of Labor, 71
UN, 30
uniform, 96
uninsured, 28
United, 5, 9, 10, 12, 13, 14, 27, 28, 29, 31, 32, 45, 49, 50, 52, 59, 64, 74, 81
United States, 5, 9, 10, 12, 14, 27, 28, 29, 31, 32, 49, 50, 52, 59, 64, 74, 81
urban, 64, 77, 78

W

wages, 16, 94
waiver, 27, 55, 60
Washington, 2, 82, 83, 96
water, 68, 78
wearing apparel, 58, 93, 94
Wisconsin, 84, 95, 96